# The Treaty of Versailles

Other books in the At Issue in History series:

# The Treaty
# of Versailles

Jeff Hay, *Book Editor*

Daniel Leone, *President*
Bonnie Szumski, *Publisher*
Scott Barbour, *Managing Editor*
Stuart Miller, *Series Editor*

 **OPPOSING VIEWPOINTS® SERIES** **AT ISSUE IN HISTORY**

Greenhaven Press, Inc.
San Diego, California

Library of Congress Cataloging-in-Publication Data

The Treaty of Versailles / Jeff Hay, book editor.
    p. cm. — (At issue in history)
    Includes bibliographical references and index.
    ISBN 0-7377-0826-3 (pbk. : alk. paper) —
ISBN 0-7377-0827-1 (lib. bdg. : alk. paper)
    1. Treaty of Versailles (1919). 2. Paris Peace Conference (1919–1920). 3. Germany—Boundaries. 4. Germany—History—1918–1933. 5. Europe—History—1918–1945. 6. World War, 1939–1945—Causes. 7. World War, 1914–1918—Peace. I. Hay, Jeff. II. Series.

D644 .T73 2002
940.3'141—dc21

                                                    2001040609

# Contents

# Foreword

Historian Robert Weiss defines history simply as "a record and interpretation of past events." Both elements—record and interpretation—are necessary, Weiss argues.

Names, dates, places, and events are the essence of history. But historical writing is not a compendium of facts. It consists of facts placed in a sequence to tell a connected story. A work of history is not merely a story, however. It also must analyze what happened and *why*—that is, it must interpret the past for the reader.

For example, the events of December 7, 1941, that led President Franklin D. Roosevelt to call it "a date which will live in infamy" are fairly well known and straightforward. A force of Japanese planes and submarines launched a torpedo and bombing attack on American military targets in Pearl Harbor, Hawaii. The surprise assault sank five battleships, disabled or sank fourteen additional ships, and left almost twenty-four hundred American soldiers and sailors dead. On the following day, the United States formally entered World War II when Congress declared war on Japan.

These facts and consequences were almost immediately communicated to the American people who heard reports about Pearl Harbor and President Roosevelt's response on the radio. All realized that this was an important and pivotal event in American and world history. Yet the news from Pearl Harbor raised many unanswered questions. Why did Japan decide to launch such an offensive? Why were the attackers so successful in catching America by surprise? What did the attack reveal about the two nations, their people, and their leadership? What were its causes, and what were its effects? Political leaders, academic historians, and students look to learn the basic facts of historical events and to read the intepretations of these events by many different sources, both primary and secondary, in order to develop a more complete picture of the event in a historical context.

In the case of Pearl Harbor, several important questions surrounding the event remain in dispute, most notably the role of President Roosevelt. Some historians have blamed his policies for deliberately provoking Japan to attack in order to propel America into World War II; a few have gone so far as to accuse him of knowing of the impending attack but not informing others. Other historians, examining the same event, have exonerated the president of such charges, arguing that the historical evidence does not support such a theory.

The Greenhaven At Issue in History series recognizes that many important historical events have been interpreted differently and in some cases remain shrouded in controversy. Each volume features a collection of articles that focus on a topic that has sparked controversy among eyewitnesses, contemporary observers, and historians. An introductory essay sets the stage for each topic by presenting background and context. Several chapters then examine different facets of the subject at hand with readings chosen for their diversity of opinion. Each selection is preceded by a summary of the author's main points and conclusions. A bibliography is included for those students interested in pursuing further research. An annotated table of contents and thorough index help readers to quickly locate material of interest. Taken together, the contents of each of the volumes in the Greenhaven At Issue in History series will help students become more discriminating and thoughtful readers of history.

# Introduction

World War I, fought from 1914 to 1918, was to be "the war to end wars," in the words of America's then president Woodrow Wilson. An idealist, Wilson could hope for nothing less. The war had been the most devastating in human history. Virtually an entire generation of Europe's young men was killed or wounded on its battlefields, and even civilians were killed in the millions. Much of Europe's productive capacity—its farms, factories, and coal mines—lay in ruins at war's end. The war opened the door to political upheaval as well; Russia's autocratic czar was overthrown in 1917 and was ultimately replaced by Bolsheviks who preached revolutionary communism. Elsewhere, the ethnic patchwork of southern and eastern Europe lay torn by groups who wanted to assert their nationalism as the powerful empires of Russia, Austria-Hungary, and the Ottoman Turks collapsed. Indeed, World War I effectively destroyed Europe's nineteenth-century order, although that notion was unclear to the world's leaders and diplomats, who gathered in Paris in early 1919 to restore, they hoped, peace and the familiar structure to the world.

The focus of the Paris Peace Conference was on creating the treaty with the defeated German empire, the eventual Treaty of Versailles. However, the acknowledged heads of the Allied and associative powers, as the winners called themselves—the "Big Three"—Wilson of the United States, Premier Georges Clemenceau of France, and Prime Minister David Lloyd George of Great Britain, differed greatly on their goals for the peace. Their negotiations were acrimonious and often seemed, to observers, shortsighted and pointless. Moreover, and contrary to the custom of such peace conferences, German representatives played no part in the negotiations although Germans claimed that they signed the armistice ending World War I on the expectation of being treated fairly and with the respect due a major power. The Treaty of Versailles, consequently, was a slapped-together affair that few were happy with and that certain observers, such as Marshal Ferdinand Foch, the French officer and supreme commander of Allied forces, were certain would lead to another war.

Foch was right. Instead of being the war to end wars, World War I segued easily into World War II, an even more devastating conflict. Wilson, Clemenceau, and Lloyd George failed to create a peaceful and orderly Europe in Paris in 1919. The Treaty of Versailles, as well as the accompanying treaties with Austria, Hungary, Bulgaria, and the Ottoman Empire (World War I's other losers), created new and sometimes unrealistic national borders, fostered ethnic rivalries, and imposed impossible economic demands on the defeated powers. Perhaps most importantly, the treaty embittered and humiliated Germany to the point that rabble rousers such as Adolf Hitler, the future Nazi dictator who served as a German army corporal from 1914 to 1918, preached vengeance against those who proposed and accepted the "dictated peace" of 1919.

The Big Three (who sometimes shared their stage with a fourth, Orlando Vittorio of Italy) came to the Paris Peace Conference with, to their minds, honorable and reasonable expectations. In many ways these expectations were built on the diplomatic and political experiences of nineteenth-century Europe, according to which powerful nations should indirectly police one another in order to maintain a rough balance of power. The last great European peace conference, 1815's Congress of Vienna at the close of the Napoleonic Wars, established the principle that peace would be maintained by such a balance among the major nations: Great Britain, France, Prussia, the Austrian Empire, Russia, and even the Turkish Ottoman Empire. To a great degree the balance-of-power principle succeeded. Between 1815 and 1914 there were no major European wars, only smaller-scale conflicts such as the Crimean War between Russia and a Franco-British alliance in the 1850s and the Franco-Prussian War of 1870.

By the late 1800s, however, new factors threatened the balance of power. Great Britain's empire expanded across the globe, as did its control of the seas and of international trade. Ottoman domination of southeastern Europe collapsed, and Russia and Austria, by then the dual monarchy of Austria-Hungary, stepped in to fill the void. Italy's unification in 1864 added another major power to the equation, and France sought in various ways to maintain its status as the dominant military and cultural force on the continent.

The rise of the German empire, however, proved to be the greatest threat to the arrangements of 1815. Under the guidance of Prussia, which seemed to outsiders to possess a culture and organization that was excessively militaristic, various German-speaking states in central Europe began to come together. Moreover, Prussian chancellor Otto von Bismarck did not hesitate to instigate small wars along the way; his forces defeated Denmark in 1864, Austria in 1866, and France in 1870. Moreover, von Bismarck was little concerned with balances of power. He preferred to assert German might, believing (along with many others) that it was Germany's destiny to dominate Europe.

The French, for their part, never forgot the humiliations of the Franco-Prussian War of 1870, which effectively completed the process of German unification. In a short six weeks the French army, considered the best in Europe, was forced to surrender as the French emperor, Napoléon III, abdicated and fled to exile in England. From this unexpected position of strength, the Prussians dictated harsh treaty terms that France was in no position to refuse. France was forced, among other things, to surrender to Germany the rich and mostly French-speaking border provinces of Alsace and Lorraine. And in a ceremony overflowing with symbolism and which Clemenceau remembered bitterly, Kaiser Wilhelm I, the Prussian king and head of the royal House of Hohenzollern, was crowned emperor of Germany in the Hall of Mirrors at Versailles, the palace of the long-gone French kings. It took place on January 18, 1871.

World War I itself was the result of the collapse of Europe's balance-of-power system. After 1871 national rivalries intensified as European nations began to act as if they were engaged in a struggle for survival instead of accepting the fact that they had to live with one another. Competitions along various lines sprang up: for colonies, for industry, for diplomatic influence, and, most ominously, an arms race involving Great Britain, France, and Germany. Although Britain and France in fact played similar games, both blamed Germany for instigating most of the conflicts that finally led to the outbreak of war in August 1914. Germany, others claimed, did not behave fairly or honorably. Instead, the Kaiser's empire seemed to go out of its way to establish secret alliances and calculate moves that would inevitably alienate the other powers. On two occasions, for instance, Germany appeared willing to go to war over Morocco, which most acknowledged as lying within the French sphere of influence. Moreover, the German navy matched and then surpassed Britain's capacity to build large warships known as dreadnoughts. To British eyes, such a move could only be directed at the British overseas empire. As a consequence of these apparent provocations, Britain and France agreed to support one another against Germany; for its part, Germany allied itself with Austria. Earlier alliances had guaranteed French support of Russia as well as Turkish support of certain of Austria's interests. World War I, then, was fought between the so-called entente powers of Great Britain, France, Russia, and later the United States, and the central powers of Germany, Austria-Hungary, and Ottoman Turkey.

Although all combatants were convinced they were strong enough to win the war quickly, World War I soon settled into what seemed an interminable quagmire. Millions of soldiers perished for little territorial gain, as senior officers proved unable to adapt nineteenth-century strategies to twentieth-century technologies such as machine guns, aircraft, and poison gas. At the Battle of Verdun in 1916, 700,000 French and German soldiers died with no meaningful achievement on either side. At the Battle of the Somme that same year, 60,000 British soldiers died in a single day, while over 1 million combatants were killed altogether. The futility of trench warfare was not limited to the western front in France and Belgium either, as over 500,000 "Anzacs"—Allied troops from Australia and New Zealand—perished in a misguided effort to take the Turkish peninsula of Gallipoli.

In February 1917 ill-led and ill-equipped Russian troops, many of them sick of the pointlessness of the war, joined many of their nation's workers and peasants in an event that was to bear greatly on the Paris Peace Conference. This Russian Revolution ultimately led to the takeover by the Bolsheviks, Russia's revolutionary Communists. V.I. Lenin, the Bolshevik leader, claimed to support an international Communist revolution, and his successes emboldened Communists in central and eastern Europe. Morever, and much to the distress of the western Allies,

Lenin took Russia out of World War I by signing a separate peace with the Germans, the Treaty of Brest-Litovsk. The treaty's terms were extremely harsh, as the negotiators at Versailles later pointed out. In order to secure the ceasefire with Germany, Lenin was forced to give up millions of square miles of territory and to pay the Germans a huge sum in reparations.

The year 1917 also saw the entrance of the United States of America into World War I on the side of the western Allies. Few Americans were convinced in 1914 that they should get involved in the endless conflicts of Europe, but President Wilson persistently argued that fighting was in America's interests, as the war would end up making "the world safe for democracy." The hundreds of thousands of American troops who began to arrive in the summer of 1917 seemed to bring about the turning point of the war. At the very least, the arrival of Americans seemed to break the war's stalemate.

*Hundreds gathered in the Hall of Mirrors to witness the signing of the Treaty of Versailles, which officially ended World War I.*

Sure that the entente powers would win, Wilson developed his "Fourteen Points" as a statement of America's war aims as well as a reflection of his general hopes for world peace, and he described them in a speech given in January

1918. The Fourteen Points demonstrated Wilson's faith in general principles ranging from open diplomacy to free trade to general disarmament. A number of the Fourteen Points supported the principle of national self-determination, arguing specifically for the creation of new nations in central and eastern Europe. It was the fourteenth, however, that appeared closest to Wilson's heart, and it turned out to be one of the greatest sources of contention at the Paris Peace Conference. In it, Wilson called for the establishment of an international body, the League of Nations, to "guarantee . . . political independence and territorial integrity to great and small states alike." Wilson hoped that such a league would make it possible for nations to settle their differences at the conference table rather than on the battlefield and thereby prevent a sequel of World War I. During the treaty negotiations Wilson refused to back down on the creation of the league, although he insisted, to the dismay of more practically minded diplomats, that this international body should never be given the ability to field its own armies since, he argued, such a force would contradict the league's initial goal of preserving peace. In the end, and rather awkwardly, the covenant establishing the League of Nations became incorporated into the Treaty of Versailles, forever linking the league with the harsh German settlement that accompanied its founding.

World War I ended in November 1918 with the signing of an armistice that was to take effect "on the eleventh hour of the eleventh day of the eleventh month." Calculating that his best chances for a favorable peace settlement lay with Wilson, Prince Max of Baden, Germany's leader at the time, asked the Americans for a peace based on the Fourteen Points. Wilson and the Allies agreed, happy to win the war without an extended invasion of Germany.

The last days of the war, however, introduced political chaos into Germany, and that situation was soon repeated in much of eastern and central Europe. On November 9 Kaiser Wilhelm II, the grandson of the autocrat who had been crowned emperor of Germany in 1871, abdicated and fled to Holland. A new government was formed by the mildly leftist Social Democratic Party in Weimar, a city in eastern Germany. From the beginning, the new Weimar Republic was faced with grave instability. The loyalty of the army was questionable; indeed the army hoped to avoid shame by forcing civilian politicians to accept both the armistice—in effect a simple cease-fire—and later the peace treaty. Meanwhile, street warfare quickly broke out between monarchist and militarist "Freikorps" troops, often led by disgruntled army officers, and Communist "Spartacists," who sought to bring bolshevism to postwar Germany. Even German unification seemed to be in question as some states considered breaking away from the militaristic Prussians. In one instance, rebels in Bavaria managed to establish a short-lived Bavarian Socialist Republic.

Elsewhere in Europe, instability and poverty reigned. Productive land lay in ruins from France to Russia, and industry and agriculture stood still. Those who had survived the war faced starvation and poverty only to confront a new threat: an international flu epidemic that killed millions in 1918 and 1919. Ethnic groups in the former Russian, Austrian, and Turkish empires took Wilson's Fourteen Points at face value and sought to invent new nations or reestablish old ones. And everywhere, Bolsheviks and their sympathizers struggled against those who hoped to restore some semblance of the old order.

It was into this environment that those staunch representatives of the old order—Clemenceau, Lloyd George, and Wilson—arrived on January 18, 1919, the anniversary of France's 1871 humiliation at German hands. Clemenceau, of course, chose the date intentionally. Accompanying the Big Three and their armies of advisers were representatives of nations and colonies from across the globe, as all were aware that the Paris Peace Conference would reorganize the world. New nations were to be created, colonial empires were to be reshuffled, and different organizations and peoples sought their share of the spoils.

The conference's greatest issue, however, remained the peace with Germany. Clemenceau favored harsh terms. He continually reminded negotiators that he had seen Germany invade France twice during his lifetime. He was not going to allow it to happen again, and he advocated extreme measures to restrict Germany's war-making capacity. French public opinion, in addition, demanded harsh terms. Lloyd George's highest priority was to prevent a German threat to the British overseas empire. Beyond that he was willing to compromise and appeared to believe that Germany should properly remain a major European power. The British prime minister however, like the French premier, had to answer to public opinion at home. Many Britons, sick of the privations of war, wanted Germany to pay for its crimes.

Wilson remained devoted to his ideals, especially his goal of the creation of the League of Nations. Provided Clemenceau and Lloyd George agreed to the league, Wilson seemed willing to bend on other matters even if they contradicted other of the Fourteen Points, such as the principle of national self-determination. For instance, Clemenceau wanted Germany to lose some of its territory or alternatively to face a long-term foreign occupation. In the end, Wilson capitulated, mostly to Clemenceau, although he got his League of Nations.

The final version of the Treaty of Versailles, so hastily assembled that few had actually seen it in its entirety, was presented to Germany's representatives on May 7. The Germans, who, again, took no part in negotiations, would be forced to accept a number of humiliating terms. They had to return Alsace-Lorraine to France, first of all. Other portions of German territory would be granted, given certain conditions were met, to Denmark and Poland. Furthermore, Germany was to accept a French occupation of the Rhineland for fifteen years while the bulk of the production of the coal-rich Saarland would go directly to France.

In a bid to discourage German militarism, the treaty also limited the size of the German army and navy and forbade the nation from possessing an air force. Observers noted that these provisions left Germany with an army large enough to quell internal disturbances but nothing more. Germany would be unable to stop an outside invasion. Beyond this, Kaiser Wilhelm II was to be captured and given over to the Allies as a war criminal.

Perhaps most galling to the Germans, however, was Article 231 of the treaty, the infamous War Guilt clause. It required Germany to accept full responsibility for starting World War I and to pay reparations to Britain, France, and other countries, the amounts of which were to be later determined by a reparations commission. From the Germans' perspective, Article 231 was hard to accept because they believed that they had fought a just and honorable war whose origins were European wide. Certainly, they claimed, they bore little more responsibility for the war than France, Russia, or the other powers. Finally, the Germans remembered that the Allies had claimed to be at war with Kaiser Wilhelm's regime, not the German people, and the Kaiser's regime was gone. How could the Weimar Republic be asked to pay for the crimes of its predecessor?

Nonetheless, these were the terms that were presented to the chief German delegate, Count Ulrich von Brockdorff-Rantzau, on that afternoon in May. He expressed his surprise at the dictated peace treaty, as did the Weimar government's leaders when they learned of it. Many German leaders refused to accept the terms, asking von Brockdorff-Rantzau to relay their misgivings to the Big Three, who remained committed to the treaty as it stood. The treaty brought about a crisis in the Weimar government, as Chancellor Philipp Scheidemann was unable to accept its terms and resigned along with his cabinet ministers. Weimar president Friedrich Ebert soon formed another government under Gustav Bauer and asked the army whether it could conceivably take the field again should Germany refuse the peace terms. Meanwhile, the German navy lodged a protest of its own: Rather than see their ships fall into Allied hands, they abandoned and scuttled them at Scapa Flow, the British port where they had been interned.

After hearing the news of the incident at Scapa Flow, Allied commitment to the treaty hardened even further. On the evening of June 22 Wilson sent a message to the new Weimar government that "the time for discussion is passed." Germany was given a deadline of twenty-four hours to notify the Allies whether they would sign the treaty. Accepting that no realistic option existed, that the German army could not realistically fight on, and perhaps hoping the treaty terms could be later revised, Bauer notified Versailles that German representatives would arrive on June 28 to sign the treaty on behalf of the Weimar Republic.

In the end, Germany's leaders ducked personal responsibility for the defeat by sending to France two obscure cabinet ministers, Dr. Hermann Müller, the secretary for foreign affairs, and Dr. Johannes Bell, the colonial secretary. The two accompanied Clemenceau, Lloyd George, and Wilson as well as the other representatives of the allied and associative powers into the vast Hall of Mirrors at Versailles, where with little ceremony the leaders affixed their seals and signatures to the peace terms. The Treaty of Versailles, which contained the Covenant of the League of Nations, was an accomplished fact.

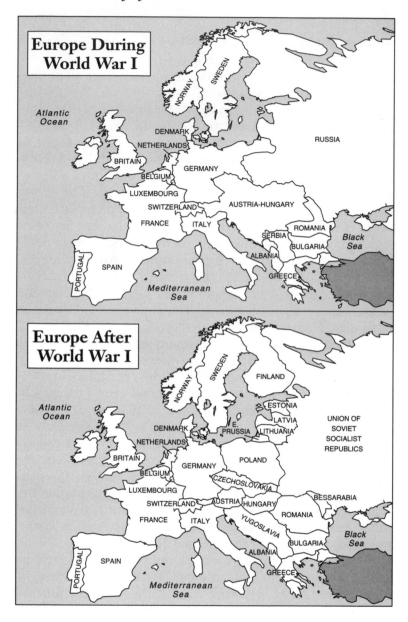

**Europe During World War I**

Atlantic Ocean

NORWAY
SWEDEN
RUSSIA
DENMARK
NETHERLANDS
BRITAIN
BELGIUM
GERMANY
LUXEMBOURG
SWITZERLAND
AUSTRIA-HUNGARY
FRANCE
ITALY
ROMANIA
SERBIA
BULGARIA
Black Sea
ALBANIA
PORTUGAL
SPAIN
GREECE
Mediterranean Sea

**Europe After World War I**

Atlantic Ocean

NORWAY
SWEDEN
FINLAND
ESTONIA
LATVIA
E. PRUSSIA
LITHUANIA
UNION OF SOVIET SOCIALIST REPUBLICS
DENMARK
NETHERLANDS
BRITAIN
BELGIUM
GERMANY
POLAND
LUXEMBOURG
CZECHOSLOVAKIA
SWITZERLAND
AUSTRIA
HUNGARY
BESSARABIA
FRANCE
ITALY
YUGOSLAVIA
ROMANIA
BULGARIA
Black Sea
ALBANIA
PORTUGAL
SPAIN
GREECE
Mediterranean Sea

Few were happy with it, however. The opinions of many observers seemed to echo those of British South African general Jan Smuts, who wrote, "Under this treaty the situation in Europe will become intolerable and a revolution must come, or again, in due course, an explosion into war. . . . The Germans behaved disgracefully in the war and deserve a hard peace. But that is no reason why the world must be thrust into ruin." There was widespread disappointment in the Big Three, who many believed had failed to take advantage of the opportunity to create a reasonable and lasting peace and whose decisions would inevitably lead to further troubles.

A young British economist, John Maynard Keynes, was among the earliest and most outspoken critics of the treaty. In 1920 he published a book, *The Economic Consequences of the Peace*, in which he predicted not only economic but also political dislocation because of the treaty's economic provisions, particularly those dealing with reparations. The reparations commission ultimately settled on amounts of money that Germany could not realistically pay without crippling its economy. And since Germany was, in Keynes's analysis, the economic engine of Europe, German poverty would spread to the rest of the continent, opening the door to starvation and, perhaps, bolshevism.

Reparations continued to be a vexing issue long after the treaty was signed. In 1923 French forces marched into Germany's industrial heartland, the Ruhr, in response to nonpayment of reparations. Germans responded by stopping work, and the Weimar government stepped up the printing of paper currency in order to maintain welfare and order and interfere with the French economy. The resulting inflation made the German mark virtually worthless; millions of marks could not buy a loaf of bread, and peoples' life savings and pensions were wiped out. Even after the American banker Charles Dawes set up a plan in 1924 to reorganize German reparations payments, many Germans began to wonder whether the Weimar Republic could ensure prosperity and order, much less make Germany strong again.

Opponents questioned the treaty's territorial provisions as well as its unrealistic economics. Although few objected to the return of Alsace-Lorraine to France, the majority of observers found the dismemberment of German territory to the east, in Poland, unreasonable and contrived. In order to ensure Polish access to the ocean, the treaty created a so-called Polish Corridor, which separated the province of East Prussia from Germany proper. In addition, French domination at various points of such regions as the Ruhr, Saarland, and the Rhineland fomented German resentment. Indeed, one of Adolf Hitler's chief rallying cries as he rose to power in the 1920s and 1930s was that the German nation should once again be free of foreign influence as well as territorially united. He found many sympathizers. Germans rejoiced when, in 1936, Hitler marched his armies into the Rhineland in blatant disregard of the treaty's territorial and military restrictions.

Ultimately, the events of the Paris Peace Conference proved the political undoing of Clemenceau, Lloyd George, and Wilson, further attesting to the fact that few had faith in their achievements. Clemenceau, despite his harsh stance, was actually attacked by the French press and rival politicians for having been too soft on Germany. Many Frenchmen had hoped, in fact, to dismember Germany by dividing it into numerous smaller states. Clemenceau had left, instead, a united Germany seething with anger and bitterness toward France. Lloyd George returned to Britain to discover that reparations payments could do little to help the ailing British economy, which was heavily in debt to the United States from the war. Although he remained a member of Parliament for many years, he lost the prime ministership in 1922.

In the United States, President Wilson failed to convince Congress to ratify the Treaty of Versailles and, contrary to his expectations, was not asked by his party to run for a third term as president in 1920. In the end, America never formally approved the treaty nor membership in the League of Nations. American absence from the league was exacerbated by the additional absences of the Soviet Union and, until 1930, Weimar Germany. With the absence of these great powers, the league could never hope to assert the influence that Wilson had envisioned when he drew up the Fourteen Points. Before long, militarists in Japan as well as Hitler in Germany and Benito Mussolini, the Italian fascist dictator, realized that the league was not a meaningful obstacle to their expansionist ambitions.

Historical assessments of the Treaty of Versailles range from those sympathetic to the reasonable intentions of the Big Three to those critical of their shortsightedness and ineptitude. Some claim that the treaty was a short-term expedient meant to appease public opinion in the aftermath of World War I, presuming that the treaty's terms would be modified or lessened as the years passed. Others criticize the French, the British, and the League of Nations for failing to take the steps necessary to enforce the treaty and the Americans for ignoring it. Throughout, World War I's victors took an unsatisfactory and weak middle course, creating a vacuum that could be filled by such willful leaders as Hitler. In the end, perhaps, as has often been suggested, the Treaty of Versailles was either too harsh or not harsh enough.

# Chapter 1

# Blaming Germany for World War I

# 1

# Tense Negotiations

Gregor Dallas

The chief negotiators of the Treaty of Versailles were President Woodrow Wilson of the United States, Premier Georges Clemenceau of France, Prime Minister David Lloyd George of Great Britain and, on the German side, a liberal aristocrat named Count Ulrich von der Brockdorff-Rantzau. In the following selection, historian Gregor Dallas describes the tenseness of the negotiations among the four as well as the intensity of emotion that surrounded the treaty. Clemenceau encouraged a hard line against Germany, while Lloyd George was more conciliatory. Meanwhile, negative German reaction to the treaty, Dallas notes, helped force Brockdorff-Rantzau's resignation as chief negotiator.

Gregor Dallas is the author of several histories of modern France.

---

So much of history is built in silence: the silence of the Paris crowds following the massacre of the Commune [in 1871], the silence of the Jews during Dreyfus riots [of the 1890s], the silence of the miners after the catastrophe of Courrières [in 1906], the silence of peasant soldiers marching to the front. But the silence that descended that Wednesday at one minute to three on the Allied delegates, secretaries and journalists in the Trianon Palace was more deliberate than these; more like the silence of an audience just before the curtain is set to rise.

There was a sudden chill of apprehension when the corner door to the garden was opened and five German reporters were escorted, by French officers, to their seats.

Excerpted from *At the Heart of a Tiger*, by Gregor Dallas. Copyright © Gregor Dallas. Reprinted by permission of the publisher, Carroll & Graf Publishers, Inc., New York.

Clemenceau, Wilson and Lloyd George sat like statues. In front of them were fourteen empty wooden chairs. The German delegation was late.

The dominant tone in the room, despite the covers of the tables, the central carpet, the ornate chairs reserved for the press, was black and white—suits, cuffs and paper. There was only one woman present, Miss Allison, a British shorthand writer, and she wore navy blue.

Five long minutes ticked by.

Then, as if provoked by a gust of wind, the main doors flew open and in came a man dressed in black and silver livery: '*Messieurs, les plénipotentiaires allemands!*' [gentlemen, the German representatives!]

A very grave column of men, all in frock-coats, followed. The count [Brockdorff-Rantzau, the head German negotiator], taking his seat directly opposite Clemenceau, had a face as white as alabaster, contrasting with his dark hair, smooth and neatly parted down the middle. To his right sat a copiously bearded Doctor Otto Landsberg, a lawyer and prominent member of the Reichstag; he was a bigger man than the count. To his left was the German postmaster general, Johann Giesbert, calm, his expression perfectly neutral.

---

*The hour has come for the heavy settling of accounts. You have asked us for peace. We are ready to accord it to you.*

---

The instant all were seated the conference president rose. The Germans had never heard Clemenceau speak. 'Messieurs les plénipotentiaires allemands, this is perhaps neither the time nor the place for superfluous words . . .' Doctor Simons, sitting directly behind the count, found Clemenceau strangely bourgeois in spite of his 'untamable expression'. He spoke, he later told his wife, 'in short staccato sentences which he threw out as if in a concentrated anger and disdain, and which from the very outset, for the Germans, made any reply quite futile'. The correspondent for *The Times*, seated further back, described Clemenceau's attitude as one of stern courtesy'; his words were uttered 'abruptly and with characteristic decision'.

'The hour has come for the heavy settling of accounts. You have asked us for peace. We are ready to accord it to you . . .' It was a short speech and was interrupted only once for the translations into English and German.

As Paul Mantoux translated the second half of the speech into English, Brockdorff-Rantzau raised his hand, as if he wanted to speak. Mantoux continued. At the same time Paul Dutasta, general secretary of the conference, got up from his seat behind Wilson and, carrying a large printed white book, entered the rectangle to place the volume on Brockdorff-Rantzau's table. The count muttered words of thanks and pushed the book to one side. The translations continued.

Eventually Clemenceau got to his feet again and said, *'La parole est à Monsieur le comte de Brockdorff-Rantzau.'* [Count Brockdorff-Rantzau may now speak.]

## Germanic Arrogance

To the horror of everyone in the room, Brockdorff-Rantzau remained seated. One could not have invented a greater affront to the Allied powers. The crouched figure of the count at his table created more of an impression on the reporters behind him than anything he said in the speech which followed; days, weeks and months would be spent searching for an explanation for this most undiplomatic behaviour. The *Times* correspondent reported that 'Count Brockdorff-Rantzau appeared to be suffering considerably.' The story circulated in the British delegation that his sufferings were so great that his legs were actually paralysed, that he was physically incapable of standing. Lloyd George offered a similar explanation in his memoirs. But Brockdorff-Rantzau himself denied it. So did his biographer. And so, most significantly, did Walter Simons in a letter to his wife written only three days after the event. He claims that the count had informed him just prior to the meeting that he would not stand; he had seen plans of the converted restaurant in the French press, which described the German delegation's table as the *banc des accusés* [bench of the accused, as in a courtroom], and he was not going to be seen as responding to the demand, 'The prisoner will stand up.' Nor was Clemenceau much moved by reports of the count's sufferings; in 1929 he still speaks of the 'Germanic arrogance' (*'jactance germanique'*) of Brockdorff-Rantzau.

Brockdorff-Rantzau donned a pair of horn-rimmed

spectacles to read his typed speech in German. Having learned that there would be no face-to-face negotiations the German delegation had decided that some spoken comment at the time of the treaty presentation was in order. The speech had gone through several drafts which had passed between Versailles, the government in Weimar and another panel of experts in Berlin. The delegation had entered the Trianon Palace equipped with a short speech and a long speech. In the end, Brockdorff-Rantzau went for the long speech.

He began by saying that his country was 'under no illusion as to the extent of our defeat and the degree of our want of power,' but the spirit of the speech indicated that he was not here to plea; he intended to be treated on terms of absolute equality. He paused after each sentence to have his words translated into French and English. The interpreters sat behind him. 'We can't hear anything,' said Clemenceau after the first French phrase. He requested that the interpreters be brought before the president's table. With grace, they stood up and worked their way through the tables of the Serbian, Czech, Rumanian, Greek and Japanese delegations until they reached the small access to the rectangle just west of the Canadian delegation. Then, before the Big Three, they repeated the first sentence. The *Times* correspondent noted that the translations were in 'very German French and very American English'. Other sources indicate that the French was terrible but that the English was in fact good.

> *Clemenceau replied, "I am going to put my piece of paper under his nose saying, 'That's where you are going to sign.'"*

Phrase by phrase, the speech continued. '*Wir kennen die Macht des Haßes, die uns hier entgegentritt . . .*' '*Nous connaissons la puissance de la haine que nous rencontrons ici . . .*' '*We are aware of the power of hatred that we are confronted with here . . .*' Lloyd George, toying with the black ribbon of his pince-nez glasses, seemed to find the whole procedure rather amusing. Bonar Law yawned. Wilson earnestly took notes. Some said Clemenceau had a slight smile on his face, others that his complexion turned red. Did Lloyd George really snap an ivory paper knife in two? For a man whose knees were supposedly shaking out of control, Brockdorff-Rantzau made quite an impression. Even the *Times* correspondent, after noting that 'Count Rantzau has not a very pleasing voice,' admitted that his 'language was vigorous' and that 'he made his remarks in the level tone of a man who is not going to allow any discussion or questioning'.

Walter Simons thought the count's speech was delivered with a voice that was 'remarkably calm, precise and curt'. But it was difficult to listen. His eyes wandered to the big window on his right, for just outside there was a magnificent cherry tree in full bloom. He later confessed to his wife that this was the 'only reality'. Sitting there, as the translations droned on, he thought to himself, 'This cherry tree and its kind will still be blooming when the states whose representatives gathered here exist no longer.'

## Germans Defend Their Position

Still the speech went on. Germany had committed errors, especially in Belgium, but no nation was innocent. Before even studying the terms lying in front of him—in truth, these terms contained no surprises for a news-reading man—he was ready with his argument against German 'guilt'. 'The imperialism of all the European states has chronically poisoned the international situation.' The Allies were apparently still committing atrocities: 'Several hundreds of thousands of non-combatants who have died since 11 November as a result of the blockade have been killed with premeditation.' Perhaps this was where the paper knife snapped. 'How are you going to respond to him?' whispered Lloyd George to Clemenceau. Clemenceau replied, 'I am going to put my piece of paper under his nose saying, "That's what you are going to sign."'

Then came the argument of the Fourteen Points: 'We are not without protection [for] we have one you have provided yourselves: it is the right guaranteed us by the treaty on the principles of peace.' Then the Bolshevik menace: 'The collapse of the German people would bring incurable devastation to the economic life of Europe.' Brockdorff-Rantzau finished his speech by saying that 'We are going to examine the document you have presented us with good will and with the hope that all will be able to contribute to the final result of our meeting.'

'There are no other observations?' asked Clemenceau. The count replied, 'No.' Clemenceau declared, 'The session is then closed.'

The German delegation rose and filed slowly out, but not before Brockdorff-Rantzau had committed one final indignity: pausing at the door, he lit a cigarette.

The German press reacted in outrage to the terms of the 'Conditions of Peace'. *'Unerträglich! Unerfüllbar! Unannehmbar!'* ('Intolerable! Unattainable! Unacceptable!') was the president's terse formula, reiterated in every journal throughout the land. Germany was to lose over a third of her coal fields, three quarters of her iron deposits, one third of her blast furnaces and all of her merchant navy. On top of that were the reparations. Only the year before the nation had been convinced she was winning the war. For many the armistice came as a shock. Was this not an agreement between equals? Had the army really been beaten? In the National Assembly, temporarily back in Berlin, the deputies sang *Deutschland über alles.* Even the Socialists were united, save Hugo Haase, who dismayed his colleagues with the reminder that the Treaty of Brest Litovsk had been no kinder to Russia.

## A Final German Hope

There was one popular hope: the Allies would be divided. An editorial in the Munich *Allgemeine Zeitung* confidently announced on 18 May, 'Lloyd George apparently already senses the labour-pains of the new times and no longer has his whole heart in this politics of power, hate and revenge, which only in Clemenceau and his accomplices finds support.'

That was also the fond dream of the delegation in Versailles, which had set immediately to work on written 'observations' on the terms presented. But they got lost in details. The German delegation contained proportionately more specialists than any other body attending the conference; the majority were doctors and *'Geheimräte'* [State Police]. It was also a constantly changing assembly of specialists. When one group was no longer needed it would return to Germany to be replaced by another. Between 9 and 29 May (the fifteen-day deadline was extended by a week) the Allies were bombarded with notes contesting virtually every article in the treaty. In the process Brockdorff-Rantzau's principal diplomatic objective, emphasising the Fourteen Points and the Bolshevik menace, became blurred. The delegation also incorrectly believed that time was on its side, grossly overestimating the extent of social troubles and political divisions within the Allied countries.

None the less, the *Allgemeine Zeitung* and its kind were correct on one point: Lloyd George was hesitant. From its earliest days the new German regime was looked upon by Lloyd George as the only possible alternative to a Soviet government, and for this reason he believed it should be strengthened. In March and April British officials had been visiting Brockdorff-Rantzau to assure him that 'the British government had no intention whatever to destroy Germany' but rather 'wished for her reconstruction and prosperity'. As the German notes accumulated in May Lloyd George began to have second thoughts about the terms so painfully negotiated with the Allies; in early June he summoned virtually his whole cabinet to Paris. After two days of meetings his government issued an ultimatum, not to Germany but to the Allies, demanding that crucial elements of the treaty be revised. The American delegation was divided, but Woodrow Wilson took a stand against revision. 'The time to consider all these questions was when we were writing the treaty,' he said, and concluded, 'Well, the Lord be with us.' As for Clemenceau, he commented, 'We do not have to beg pardon for our victory.' He reminded his Allies that his whole policy at the conference had been to maintain a 'close union with Great Britain and America', and the result of this was that he had been criticised at home for being weak and inadequate. 'If I fall,' he warned, 'you will be faced with even greater differences of opinion than those which separate us today.' Slight modifications were made to the terms (on reparations and a plebiscite in Upper Silesia) then the ultimatum was turned on Germany.

Brockdorff-Rantzau resigned, Scheidemann's government fell, there was very nearly a military coup, but in the end, three hours before Allied troops were set to march, Germany gave notice that she would sign. The actual signing in the Hall of Mirrors, on 28 June, was mere ceremony.

So for the moment the revisionists and the appeasers were silenced, the Allies remained united and the principle of international responsibility was inscribed on vellum.

# 2

# A Harsh Treaty with Germany Is Fully Justified

The Allied and Associated Powers

The following selection is from an official Allied response to German complaints, prior to signing, that the Treaty of Versailles was unnecessarily harsh and unfair. The Germans felt that they had fought a just and honorable war, which they had not begun, and that the German people should not be made to pay the price for their army's failures on the battlefield. Moreover, the imperial government of Kaiser Wilhelm II, which led Germany before and during World War I, had been toppled and replaced by the Weimar Republic. German representatives wondered why the new government should be held responsible for the actions of the old. The Allied response addresses these complaints and goes on to assert that Germany's crimes demanded the sort of treatment laid out in the Treaty.

---

T he protest of the German delegation shows that they fail to understand the position in which Germany stands today. They seem to think that Germany has only to "make sacrifices in order to obtain peace," as if this were but the end of some mere struggle for territory and power. The Allied and Associated Powers therefore feel it necessary to begin their reply by a clear statement of the judgment of the world, which has been forged by practically the whole of civilized mankind.

In the view of the Allied and Associated Powers the war

Excerpted from *The War, the World, and Wilson,* by George Creel (New York: Harper & Brothers, 1920).

which began on the 1st of August, 1914, was the greatest crime against humanity and the freedom of the peoples that any nation calling itself civilized has ever consciously committed. For many years the rulers of Germany, true to the Prussian tradition, strove for a position of dominance in Europe. They were not satisfied with that growing prosperity and influence to which Germany was entitled, and which all other nations were willing to accord her, or the society of free and equal position.

## Germany Planned to Dominate Europe

They required that they should be able to dictate and tyrannize over a subservient Europe, as they dictated and tyrannized over a subservient Germany. In order to attain their ends they used every channel through which to educate their own subjects in the doctrine that might was right in international affairs. They never ceased to expand German armaments by land and sea, and to propagate the falsehood that it was necessary because Germany's neighbors were jealous of her prosperity and power. She sought to sow hostilities and suspicion instead of friendship between nations.

They developed a system of espionage and intrigue through which they were enabled to stir up international rebellion and unrest, and even to make secret offensive preparations within the territory of their neighbors, whereby they might, when the moment came, strike them down with greater certainty and ease. They kept Europe in a ferment by threats of violence, and when they found that their neighbors were resolved to resist their arrogant will they determined to assert their predominance in Europe by force.

As soon as their preparations were complete, they encouraged a subservient ally to declare war on Serbia at forty-eight hours' notice, a war involving the control of the Balkans, which they knew could not be localized and which was bound to unchain a general war. In order to make doubly sure, they refused every attempt at conciliation and conference until it was too late and the World War was inevitable for which they had plotted and for which alone among the nations they were adequately equipped and prepared.

Germany's responsibility, however, is not confined to having planned and started the war. She is no less responsible for the savage and inhuman manner in which it was conducted. Though Germany was herself a guarantor of Belgium, the rulers of Germany violated their solemn promise to respect the neutrality of this unoffending people. Not content with this, they deliberately carried out a series of promiscuous shootings and burnings with the sole object of terrifying the inhabitants into submission by the very frightfulness of their action.

They were the first to use poisonous gas, notwithstanding the appalling suffering it entailed. They began the bombing and long-distance shelling of towns for no military object, but solely for the purpose of reducing the morale of their opponents by striking at their women and children. They commenced the submarine campaign, with its piratical challenge to international law and its destruction of great numbers of innocent passengers and sailors in mid-ocean, far from succor, at the mercy of the winds and waves, and the yet more ruthless submarine crews.

---

*[Germans] kept Europe in a ferment by threats of violence, and when they found that their neighbors were resolved to resist their arrogant will they determined to assert their predominance in Europe by force.*

---

They drove thousands of men and women and children with brutal savagery into slavery in foreign lands. They allowed barbarities to be practised against their prisoners of war from which the most uncivilized people would have recoiled.

The conduct of Germany is almost unexampled in human history. The terrible responsibility which lies at her doors can be seen in the fact that not less than 7,000,000 dead lie buried in Europe, while more than 20,000,000 others carry upon them the evidence of wounds and suffering, because Germany saw fit to gratify her lust for tyranny by a resort to war.

## The Victorious Allies Demand Justice

Justice, therefore, is the only possible basis for the settlement of the accounts of this terrible war. Justice is what the German delegation asks for, and says that Germany has been promised. But it must be justice for all. There must be justice for the dead and wounded, and for those who have been orphaned and bereaved, that Europe might be free from Prussian despotism. There must be justice for the peoples who now stagger under war debts which exceed $30,000,000,000 that liberty might be saved. There must be justice for those millions whose homes and lands and property German savagery has spoliated and destroyed.

This is why the Allied and Associated Powers have insisted as a cardinal feature of the treaty that Germany must undertake to make reparation to the very uttermost of her power, for reparation for wrongs inflicted is of the essence of justice. That is why they insist that those individuals who are most clearly responsible for German aggression and for those acts of barbarism and inhumanity which have disgraced the German conduct of the war must be handed over to justice, which has not been meted out to them at home. That, too, is why Germany must submit for a few years to certain special disabilities and arrangements.

Germany has ruined the industries, the mines, and the machinery of neighboring countries, not during battle, but with the deliberate and calculated purpose of enabling her own industries to seize their markets before their industries could recover from the devastation thus wantonly inflicted upon them. Germany has despoiled her neighbors of everything she could make use of or carry away. Germany has destroyed the shipping of all nations on the high seas, where there was no chance of rescue for the passengers and crews.

> *The conduct of Germany is almost unexampled in human history.*

It is only justice that restitution should be made, and that these wronged peoples should be safeguarded for a time from the competition of a nation whose industries are intact and have even been fortified by machinery stolen from occupied territories.

If these things are hardships for Germany, they are hardships which Germany has brought upon herself. Somebody must suffer for the consequences of the war. Is it to be Germany or the peoples she has wronged? Not to do justice to all concerned would only leave the world open to fresh calamities. If the German people themselves, or any other nation, are to be deterred from following the footsteps of Prussia; if mankind is to be lifted out of the belief that war for selfish ends is legitimate to any state; if the old era is to be left behind, and nations as well as individuals are to be brought beneath the reign of law, even if there is to be early reconciliation and appeasement—it will be because those responsible for concluding the war have had the courage to see that justice is not deflected for the sake of a convenient peace.

## The German People Supported Their Warlike Leaders

It is said that the German revolution ought to make a difference, and that the German people are not responsible for the policy of the rulers whom they have thrown from power. The Allied and Associated Powers recognize and welcome the change. It represents great hope for peace and a new European order in the future, but it cannot affect the settlement of the war itself.

---

*Somebody must suffer for the consequences of the war. Is it to be Germany or the peoples she has wronged?*

---

The German revolution was stayed until the German armies had been defeated in the field and all hope of profiting by a war of conquest had vanished. Throughout the war, as before the war, the German people and their representatives supported the war, voted the credits, subscribed to the war loans, obeyed every order, however savage, of their government. They shared the responsibility for the policy of their government, for at any moment, had they willed it, they could have reversed it.

Had that policy succeeded they would have acclaimed it with the same enthusiasm with which they welcomed the outbreak of the war. They cannot now pretend, having changed their rulers after the war was lost, that it is justice that they should escape the consequences of their deeds.

In conclusion, the Allied and Associated Powers must make it clear that this letter constitute[s] their last word.

They have examined the German observations and counter-proposals with earnest attention and care. They have, in consequence, made important modifications in the draft treaty, but in its principles they stand by it.

They believe that it is not only a just settlement of the Great War, but that it provides the basis upon which the peoples of Europe can live together in friendship and equality. At the same time it creates the machinery for the peaceful adjustment of all international problems by discussion and consent, and whereby the settlement of 1919 itself can be modified from time to time to suit new facts and new conditions as they arise.

# 3

# German Leaders Wanted to Reject the Treaty

Philipp Scheidemann

The following passage is from the memoirs of Philipp Scheidemann, the first prime minister of the Weimar Republic, the
regime which governed Germany after the abdication of
Kaiser Wilhelm II on November 9, 1918. In it Scheidemann
remembers the violent reaction of his government to the terms
of the Treaty of Versailles, presented by the western allies to
German delegates on May 7, 1919. Quoting one of his
speeches from that era, Scheidemann emphasizes the widespread sense in Germany that the allies, instead of a reasonable
peace, sought simple revenge against a hated adversary. Unable to either modify the treaty terms or force his government
to accept them, Scheidemann resigned as prime minister on
June 20, leaving the task to a new leader.

T he delegates who went to Versailles at the end of April
with Count Brockdorff-Rantzau, the Foreign Secretary, as President, were Landsberg, Minister of Justice, Gies-
berts, Postmaster-General, Leinert, President of the Diet,
Dr. Melchior-Hamburg, the banker, and the International
Law Professor, Schücking, a member of the National Assembly. The Peace Treaty handed to these delegates on 7th
May was the most iniquitous piece of work ever produced by
blind hatred and senseless fury. Prince Max's Government,
in its telegraphic communications with Wilson, took ex-
pressly as its basis the points formulated by the President of
the United States. These points were as valid with the En-

Excerpted from *The Making of New Germany: The Memoirs of Philipp Scheidemann*,
translated by J.E. Michell, vol. 2 (New York: D. Appleton, 1929). Copyright 1928
by Carl Reissner.

tente as their solemn assurances that "the Entente was not waging war against the German people, but against Kaiserism and Prussian militarism." Although the Kaiser had fled, and was therefore non-existent, although Prussian militarism lay prostrate on the ground, while the countries of the Entente were armed to the teeth, although a Parliament elected by the people and a Government with a Social Democratic President and Premier represented the German nation—in spite of all this, here was this mad dictated Treaty, by which a people of seventy millions was to be enslaved and shorn of its honour and defence for scores of years.

"Never! never!" was the despairing unanimous cry throughout the land. "Never!" in unimportant coteries could be heard mutterings of doubt. "Never!" said Erzberger [the leader of the Catholic Center Party] in the early days when irresponsible orators pleaded for immediate acceptance. The heavy roller went many times over this dictated Peace. . . .

## Refusing the Treaty

On the afternoon of 12th May a meeting of the National Assembly took place in the new Aula [Assembly Hall] of the University. As Prime Minister, I spoke on behalf of the Government on the Versailles Treaty. A few extracts from the speech may be given here:

"On strange premises in emergency quarters, the representatives of the nation have met together, like a last remnant of loyal men, at a time when the Fatherland is in the gravest danger. All are present except the Alsace-Lorrainers, from whom the right of being here represented has been taken away, as well as the right of exercising their privilege of self-determination as free men.

"When I see lined up here the representatives of German stock and nationality, men chosen from the Rhineland, the Saar Basin, West and East Prussia, Posen, Silesia and Memel, side by side with Parliamentarians from countries that are not threatened and men from countries that are, who, if the will of our enemies becomes law, will now for the last time meet Germans as Germans, I am conscious of being one with you in spirit at this sad and solemn hour when we have only one command to obey: We must hold together. We must stick together. We are one flesh and one blood, and he who tries to separate us cuts with a murderous knife into the live flesh of the German people. To preserve the life of our people is our highest duty.

"We are chasing no nationalistic phantoms; no question of prestige and no thirst of power have any part or lot in our deliberations. For country and people we must save life—a bare, poor life now, when everyone feels the throttling hand on his throat. Let me speak without mincing my words; what lies at the root of our deliberations is this thick book [pointing to the Peace Terms], in which hundreds of paragraphs begin with 'Germany renounces—renounces—renounces'—this *malleus maleficarum* [evil witchcraft] by which the confession of our own unworthiness, the consent to our own merciless dismemberment, the agreement to our enslavement and bondage, are to be wrung and extorted from a great people—this book shall not be our law manual for the future!"

Then followed comparisons of the dictated Peace with Wilson's fourteen points, and a description of the devastating effect of the Treaty for Germany in home and foreign policy.

Then I continued:

"I ask you: who can, as an honest man, I will not say as a German, but only as an honest, straightforward man, accept such terms? What hand would not wither that binds itself and us in these fetters?" (Great applause.) "And now I've said enough, more than enough. We have made counter proposals; we shall make others. We see, with your approval, that our sacred duty lies in negotiation. This Treaty, in the opinion of the Government, cannot be accepted." (Tumultuous cheering, lasting for minutes in the Hall and galleries. The meeting rises.)

---

*The Peace Treaty handed to [the] delegates on
7th May was the most iniquitous piece of work
ever produced by blind hatred and senseless fury.*

---

"This Treaty is so impossible that I cannot yet realize the world containing such a book without millions and trillions of throats in all lands and of all parties yelling out: 'Away with this organized murder.'"

My speech ended with these words:

"We have done with fighting; we want peace. We behold in horror from the example of our enemies what convulsions a policy of force and brutal militarism have caused. With a shudder we turn our heads away from these long years of murder.

"Yes, we do. Woe to them who have conjured up the War. But threefold woe to them who postpone a real peace for a single day."

Vociferous cheers and clapping of hands followed, as per the shorthand report.

---

*"Who can, as an honest man . . . accept such terms? What hand would not wither that binds itself and us in these fetters?"*

---

For the Social Democratic Party Hermann Müller declared that the Treaty in its present form could not be accepted. Groeber said on behalf of the Centre: "We reject it." Konrad Haussmann said the same for the Democrats. Stresemann spoke for the German People's Party: "This offer is a mixed grill of French vengeance and English brutality." Haase for the Independents criticized the Treaty, but did not say it was impossible. On the other hand, his Party forthwith organized protest meetings against the no of the National Assembly. It was a bad blow for the policy of the Government that was not unanimous against the Treaty. The S.P.D. [Social Democratic Party] replied to the demonstrations of the Independents with a powerful manifesto against a treaty by force, and I added: "In the present Government no one is sitting who would be so dishonest as to promise what he knows he cannot keep. . . . We want peace, and we want it based on Wilson's points; we are ready to treat. Our whole endeavour is directed to making smooth the path to negotiations that must not deviate from what may really bring peace to the world."

I believe the conduct of no politician could have been more consistent from the very start to the bitter end.

Ebert [President of the Weimar Republic], with whom I naturally kept in close touch during these days, declared himself in perfect sympathy with my point of view. Even to foreign friends he asserted that the Treaty could in no circumstances be accepted if it were not materially improved. He also stated it publicly. I had advised him to be as definite in his language as I was forced to be as Prime Minister and was able to be on the strength of my convictions. Ebert was mortally offended, and assured me that he was just as determined as I was to say no. Next day he stood on the balcony in the Wilhelmstrasse and declared to the crowd assembled: "We will not sign this Treaty, no matter what may happen." This scene appeared in the illustrated papers together with his speech. As Ebert knew that our foreign representatives in Sweden, Denmark, Holland and Switzerland definitely expected the Treaty to be turned down, I pictured to myself the grave difficulties that would arise if Ebert really said no and resigned. I had told him and others of my friends officially that I would in no circumstances sign the Treaty, not even if the Party should object. The Party could get anybody to sign they liked; my name would not appear under any treaty in which we clearly said that the enemy could do with us whatsoever they liked because we were the scum of the earth—Germans.

# 4

# The Victorious Allies Had Contradictory Expectations

E.J. Dillon

American president Woodrow Wilson's Fourteen Points proclaimed that the peace that followed World War I should be based on the ideals of national self-determination as well as a community of nations in which disputes could be settled openly and in good faith. Other participants in the Paris Peace Conference, particularly Premier Georges Clemenceau of France, emphasized instead a harsh treaty with Germany. In the following passage, written in 1920, historian and journalist E.J. Dillon, who knew personally many of the diplomats involved, asserts that these contradictory goals made the Treaty of Versailles in its final form difficult for anyone to accept. The treaty created, Dillon notes, unrealistic and unfair territorial situations such as French domination of the German Saarland, which would inevitably lead to further conflict and was clearly contradictory to President Wilson's aims.

W ilsonianism proved to be a very different system from that of the Fourteen Points, and its author played the part not only of an interpreter of his tenets, but also of a sort of political pope alone competent to annul the force of laws binding on all those whom he should refuse to dispense from their observance. He had to do with patriotic politicians permeated with the old ideas, desirous of providing in the peace terms for the next war and striving to secure the

Excerpted from *The Inside Story of the Peace Conference*, by E.J. Dillon (New York: Harper & Brothers, 1920).

maximum of advantage over the foe presumptive, by dismembering his territory, depriving him of colonies, making him dependent on others for his supplies of raw stuffs, and artificially checking his natural growth. Nearly all of them had principles to invoke in favor of their claims and some had nothing else. And it was these tendencies which Mr. Wilson sought to combine with the ethical ideals to be incarnated in the Society of Nations. Now this was an impossible synthesis.

## The Allies Had Contradictory Expectations

The spirit of vindictiveness—for that was well represented at the Conference—was to merge and lose itself in an outflow of magnanimity; precautions against a hated enemy were to be interwoven with implicit confidence in his generosity; a military occupation would provide against a sudden onslaught, while an approach to disarmament would bear witness to the absence of suspicion. Thus Poland would discharge the function of France's ally against the Teutons in the east, but her frontiers were to leave her inefficiently protected against their future attacks from the west. Germany was dismembered, yet she was credited with self-discipline and generosity enough to steel her against the temptation to profit by the opportunity of joining together again what France had dissevered. The League of Nations was to be based upon mutual confidence and good fellowship, yet one of its most powerful future members was so distrusted as to be declared permanently unworthy to possess any overseas colonies. Germany's territory in the Saar Valley is admittedly inhabited by Germans, yet for fifteen years there is to be a foreign administration there, and at the end of it the people are to be asked whether they would like to cut the bonds that link them with their own state and place themselves under French sway, so that a premium is offered for French immigration into the Saar Valley.

Those are a few of the consequences of the mixture of the two irreconcilable principles.

That Germany richly deserved her punishment cannot be gainsaid. Her crime was without precedent. Some of its most sinister consequences are irremediable. Whole sections of her people are still unconscious not only of the magnitude, but of the criminal character, of their misdeeds. None the less there is a future to be provided for, and one of the safest provisions is to influence the potential enemy's will for evil if his power cannot be paralyzed. And this the Treaty failed to do.

---

*There is a future to be provided for, and one of the safest provisions is to influence the potential enemy's will for evil if his power cannot be paralyzed.*

---

The Germans, when they learned the conditions, discussed them angrily, and the keynote was refusal to sign the document. The financial clauses were stigmatized as masked slavery. The press urged that during the war less than one-tenth of France's territory had been occupied by their countrymen and that even of this only a fragment was in the zone of combat. The entire wealth of France, they alleged, had been estimated before the war at from three hundred and fifty milliard to four hundred milliard francs, consequently for the devastated provinces hardly more than one-twentieth of that sum could fairly be demanded as reparation, whereas the claim set forth was incomparably more. They objected to the loss of their colonies because the justification alleged—that they were disqualified to administer them because of their former cruelties toward the natives—was groundless, as the Allies themselves had admitted implicitly by offering them the right of pre-emption in the case of the Portuguese and other overseas possessions on the very eve of the war.

## French Occupation of the German Saarland

But the most telling objections turned upon the clauses that dealt with the Saar Valley. Its population is entirely German, yet the treaty-makers provided for its occupation by the French for a term of fifteen years and its transference to them if, after that term, the German government was unable to pay a certain sum in gold for the coal mines it contained. If that sum were not forthcoming the population and the district were to be handed over to France for all time, even though the former should vote unanimously for reunion with Germany. Count Brockdorff-Rantzau remarked in his note on the Treaty "that in the history of modern times there is no other example of a civilized Power obliging a state to abandon its people to foreign domination as an equivalent for a cash payment." One of the most influential press organs complained that the Treaty "bartered German men, women, and children for coal; subjected some districts with a thoroughly German population to an obligatory plebiscite under interested supervision; severed others without any consultation from the Fatherland; delivered over the proceeds of German industry to the greed of foreign capitalists for an indefinite period; . . . spread over the whole country a network of alien commissions to be paid by the German nation; withdrew streams, rivers, railways, the air service, numerous industrial establishments, the entire economic system, from the sovereignty of the German state by means either of internationalization or financial control; conferred on foreign inspectors rights such as only the satraps of absolute monarchs in former ages were empowered to exercise; in a word, they put an end to the existence of the German nation as such. Germany would become a colony of white slaves. . . ."

## Criticism of the Treaty

Fortunately for the Allies, the reproach of exchanging human beings for coal was seen by their leaders to be so damaging that they modified the odious clause that warranted it. Even the comments of the friendly neutral press were extremely pungent. They found fault with the Treaty on grounds which, unhappily, cannot be reasoned away. "Why dissimulate it?" writes the foremost of these journals; "this peace is not what we were led to expect. It dislodges the old dangers, but creates new ones. Alsace and Lorraine are, it is true, no longer in German hands, but . . . irredentism has only changed its camp. In 1914 Germany put her faith in force because she herself wielded it. But crushed down under a peace which appears to violate the promises made to her, a peace which in her heart of hearts she will never accept, she will turn toward force anew. It will stand out as the great misfortune of this Treaty that it has tainted the victory with a moral blight and caused the course of the German revolution to swerve. . . . The fundamental error of the instrument lies in the circumstance that it is a compromise between two incompatible frames of mind. It was feasible to restore peace to Europe by pulling down Germany definitely. But in order to accomplish this it would have been necessary to crush a people of seventy millions and to incapacitate them from rising to their feet again. Peace could also have been secured by the sole force of right. But in this case Germany would have had to be treated so considerately as to leave her no grievance to brood over. M. Clemenceau hindered Mr. Wilson from displaying sufficient generosity to get the moral peace, and Mr. Wilson on his side prevented M. Clemenceau from exercising severity enough to secure the material peace. And so the result, which it was easy to foresee, is a régime devoid of the real guaranties of durability."

---

*The peace conditions . . . are inacceptable from various points of view, financial, territorial, economic, social, and human.*

---

The judge of the French syndicalists [advocates of direct policitical action] was still more severe. "The Versailles peace," exclaimed M. Verfeuil, "is worse than the peace of Brest-Litovsk . . . annexations, economic servitudes, overwhelming indemnities, and a caricature of the Society of Nations—these constitute the balance of the new policy. The Deputy Marcel Cachin said: "The Allied armies fought to make this war the last. They fought for a just and lasting peace, but none of these boons has been bestowed on us. We are confronted with the failure of the policy of the one man in whom our party had put its confidence—President Wilson. The peace conditions . . . are inacceptable from various points of view, financial, territorial, economic, social, and human."

It is in this Treaty far more than in the Covenant [of the League of Nations] that the principles to which Mr. Wilson at first committed himself are in decisive issue. True, he was wont after every surrender he made during the Conference to invoke the Covenant and its concrete realization—the League of Nations—as the corrective which would set everything right in the future. But the fact can hardly be blinked that it is the Treaty and its effects that impress their character on the Covenant and not the other way round. As an eminent Swiss professor observed: "No league of nations would have hindered the Belgian people in 1830 from separating from Holland. Can the future League of Nations hinder Germany from reconstituting its geographical unity? Can it hinder the Germans of Bohemia from smiting the Czech? Can it prevent the Magyars [Hungarians], who at present are scattered, from working for their reunion?"

These potential disturbances are so many dangers to France. For if war should break out in eastern Europe, is it to be supposed that the United States, the British colonies, or even Britain herself will send troops to take part in it? Hardly. Suppose, for instance, that the Austrians, who ardently desire to be merged in Germany, proclaim their union with her, as I am convinced they will one day, does any statesman believe that democratic America will despatch troops to coerce them back? If the Germans of Bohemia secede from the Czechoslovaks or the Croats from the Serbs, will British armies cross the sea to uphold the union which those peoples repudiate? And in the name of which of the Fourteen Points would they undertake the task? That of self-determination? France's interests, and hers alone, would be affected by such changes. And France would be left to fight single-handed. For what?

It is interesting to note how the conditions imposed upon Germany were appreciated by an influential body of Mr. Wilson's American partizans who had pinned their faith to his Fourteen Points. Their view is expressed by their press organ as follows:

"France remains the strongest Power on the Continent. With her military establishment intact she faces a Germany without a general staff, without conscription, without universal military training, with a strictly limited amount of light artillery, with no air service, no fleet, with no domestic basis in raw materials for armament manufacture, with her whole western border fifty kilometers east of the Rhine demilitarized. On top of this France has a system of military alliances with the new states that touch Germany. On top of this she secured permanent representation in the Council of the League, from which Germany is excluded. On top of that economic terms which, while they cannot be fulfilled, do cripple the industrial life of her neighbor. With such a balance of forces France demands for herself a form of protection which neither Belgium, nor Poland, nor Czechoslovakia, nor Italy is granted."

# Chapter 2

# Assessments of the Treaty

# 1

# The Treaty of Versailles Encouraged Future Conflict

Winston S. Churchill

The following passage is by Winston S. Churchill, who served Britain as Lord of the Admiralty in the early years of World War I as well as Prime Minister during World War II. Writing after that second war, Churchill claimed that the Treaty of Versailles made a further conflict nearly inevitable. Its economic and territorial provisions encouraged not only resentment but also the growth of such forms of political extremism as fascism in Italy, Nazism in Germany, and Communism not only in the Soviet Union but throughout Europe. Moreover, the Treaty's architects were naive in hoping that Germany could turn itself into a democratic republic, as it had little experience of such a system. Finally, Churchill notes that America's renewed isolation greatly reduced the Treaty's credibility.

O n Armistice Day the German Armies had marched homeward in good order. "They fought well", said Marshal Foch, Generalissimo of the Allies, with the laurels bright upon his brow, speaking in soldierly mood: "let them keep their weapons". But he demanded that the French frontier should henceforth be the Rhine. Germany might be disarmed; her military system shivered in fragments; her fortresses dismantled: Germany might be impoverished; she might be loaded with measureless indemnities; she might become a prey to internal feuds: but all this would pass in

Excerpted from *The Second World War*, vol. 1: *The Gathering Storm*, by Winston S. Churchill (London: Cassell, 1948).

ten years or in twenty. The indestructible might "of all the German tribes" would rise once more and the unquenched fires of warrior Prussia glow and burn again. But the Rhine, the broad, deep, swift-flowing Rhine, once held and fortified by the French Army, would be a barrier and a shield behind which France could dwell and breathe for generations. Very different were the sentiments and views of the English-speaking world, without whose aid France must have succumbed. The territorial provisions of the Treaty of Versailles left Germany practically intact. She still remained the largest homogeneous racial block in Europe. When Marshal Foch heard of the signing of the Peace Treaty of Versailles he observed with singular accuracy: "This is not Peace. It is an Armistice for twenty years."

The economic clauses of the Treaty were malignant and silly to an extent that made them obviously futile. Germany was condemned to pay reparations on a fabulous scale. These dictates gave expression to the anger of the victors, and to the failure of their peoples to understand that no defeated nation or community can ever pay tribute on a scale which would meet the cost of modern war.

## Unreasonable Economic Demands

The multitudes remained plunged in ignorance of the simplest economic facts, and their leaders, seeking their votes, did not dare to undeceive them. The newspapers, after their fashion, reflected and emphasised the prevailing opinions. Few voices were raised to explain that payment of reparations can only be made by services or by the physical transportation of goods in wagons across land frontiers or in ships across salt water; or that when these goods arrive in the demanding countries, they dislocate the local industry except in very primitive or rigorously-controlled societies. In practice, as even the Russians have now learned, the only way of pillaging a defeated nation is to cart away any movables which are wanted, and to drive off a portion of its manhood as permanent or temporary slaves. But the profit gained from such processes bears no relation to the cost of the war. No one in great authority had the wit, ascendancy, or detachment from public folly, to declare these fundamental, brutal facts to the electorates; nor would anyone have been believed if he had. The triumphant Allies continued to assert that they would squeeze Germany "till the pips squeaked". All this had a potent bearing on the prosperity of the world and the mood of the German race.

In fact, however, these clauses were never enforced. On the contrary, whereas about £1,000 millions of German assets were appropriated by the victorious Powers, more than £500 millions were lent a few years later to Germany principally by the United States and Great Britain, thus enabling the ruin of the war to be rapidly repaired in Germany. As this apparently magnanimous process was still accompanied by the machine-made howlings of the unhappy and embittered populations in the victorious countries, and the assurances of their statesmen that Germany should be made to pay "to the uttermost farthing", no gratitude or good will was to be expected or reaped.

---

*When Marshal Foch heard of the signing of the Peace Treaty of Versailles he observed with singular accuracy: "This is not Peace. It is an Armistice for twenty years."*

---

Germany only paid, or was only able to pay, the indemnities later extorted because the United States was profusely lending money to Europe, and especially to her. In fact, during the three years 1926 to 1929 the United States was receiving back in the form of debt-instalment indemnities from all quarters about one-fifth of the money which she was lending to Germany with no chance of repayment. However, everybody seemed pleased and appeared to think this might go on forever.

History will characterise all these transactions as insane. They helped to breed both the martial curse and the "economic blizzard", of which more later. Germany now borrowed in all directions, swallowing greedily every credit which was lavishly offered her. Misguided sentiment about aiding the vanquished nation, coupled with a profitable rate of interest on these loans, led British investors to participate, though on a much smaller scale than those of the United States. Thus Germany gained the two thousand millions sterling in loans as against the one thousand millions of indemnities which she paid in one form or another by surrender of capital assets and *valuta* in foreign countries, or by juggling with the enormous American loans. All this is a sad story of complicated idiocy in the making of which much toil and virtue was consumed.

## Neither Austria Nor Germany Had the Foundation of a Democratic Republic

The second cardinal tragedy was the complete break-up of the Austro-Hungarian Empire by the Treaties of St. Germain and Trianon. For centuries this surviving embodiment of the Holy Roman Empire had afforded a common life, with advantages in trade and security, to a large number of peoples, none of whom in our own time had the strength or vitality to stand by themselves in the face of pressure from a revivified Germany or Russia. All these races wished to break away from the Federal or Imperial structure, and to encourage their desires was deemed a liberal policy. The Balkanisation of South-Eastern Europe proceeded apace, with the consequent relative aggrandisement of Prussia and the German Reich, which, though tired and war-scarred, was intact and locally overwhelming. There is not one of the peoples or provinces that constituted the Empire of the Hapsburgs to whom gaining their independence has not brought the tortures which ancient poets and theologians had reserved for the damned. The noble capital of Vienna, the home of so much long-defended culture and tradition, the centre of so many roads, rivers and railways, was left stark and starving, like a great emporium in an impoverished district whose inhabitants have mostly departed.

The victors imposed upon the Germans all the long-sought ideals of the liberal nations of the West. They were relieved from the burden of compulsory military service and from the need of keeping up heavy armaments. The enormous American loans were presently pressed upon them, though they had no credit. A democratic constitution, in accordance with all the latest improvements, was established at Weimar. Emperors having been driven out, nonentities were elected. Beneath this flimsy fabric raged the passions of the mighty, defeated, but substantially uninjured German nation. The prejudice of the Americans against monarchy, which Mr. Lloyd George made no attempt to counteract, had made it clear to the beaten Empire that it would have better treatment from the Allies as a Republic than as a Monarchy. Wise policy would have crowned and fortified the Weimar Republic with a constitudonal sovereign in the person of an infant grandson of the Kaiser, under a Council of Regency. Instead, a gaping void was opened in the national life of the German people. All the strong elements, military and feudal, which might have rallied to a constitutional monarchy and for its sake respected and sustained the new democratic and Parliamentary processes, were for the time being unhinged. The Weimar Republic, with all its liberal trappings and blessings, was regarded as an imposition of the enemy. It could not hold the loyalties or the imagination of the German people. For a spell they sought to cling as in desperation to the aged Marshal Hindenburg. Thereafter mighty forces were adrift, the void was open, and into that void after a pause there strode a maniac of ferocious genius, the repository and expression of the most virulent hatreds that have ever corroded the human breast—Corporal Hitler.

## French Fears

France had been bled white by the war. The generation that had dreamed since 1870 of a war of revenge had triumphed, but at a deadly cost in national life-strength. It was a haggard France that greeted the dawn of victory. Deep fear of Germany pervaded the French nation on the morrow of their dazzling success. It was this fear that had prompted Marshal Foch to demand the Rhine frontier for the safety of France against her far larger neighbour. But the British and American statesmen held that the absorption of German-populated districts in French territory was contrary to the Fourteen Points and to the principles of nationalism and self-determination upon which the Peace Treaty was to be based. They therefore withstood Foch and France. They gained Clemenceau by promising: first, a joint Anglo-American guarantee for the defence of France; secondly, a demilitarised zone; and thirdly, the total, lasting disarmament of Germany. Clemenceau accepted this in spite of Foch's protests and his own instincts. The Treaty of Guarantee was signed accordingly by Wilson and Lloyd George and Clemenceau. The United States Senate refused to ratify the treaty. They repudiated President Wilson's signature. And we, who had deferred so much to his opinions and wishes in all this business of peace-making, were told without much ceremony that we ought to be better informed about the American Constitution.

In the fear, anger and disarray of the French people, the rugged, dominating figure of Clemenceau, with his world-famed authority, and his special British and American contacts, was incontinently discarded. "Ingratitude towards their great men", says Plutarch, "is the mark of strong peoples". It was imprudent for France to indulge this trait when she was so grievously weakened. There was little compensating strength to be found in the revival of the group intrigues and ceaseless changes of Governments and Ministers which were the characteristic of the Third Republic, however profitable or diverting they were to those engaged in them.

---

*As Fascism sprang from Communism, so Nazism developed from Fascism.*

---

Poincaré, the strongest figure who succeeded Clemenceau, attempted to make an independent Rhineland under the patronage and control of France. This had no chance of success. He did not hesitate to try to enforce reparations on Germany by the invasion of the Ruhr. This certainly imposed compliance with the Treaties on Germany; but it was severely condemned by British and American opinion. As a result of the general financial and political disorganisation of Germany together with reparation payments during the years 1919 to 1923, the Mark rapidly collapsed. The rage aroused in Germany by the French occupation of the Ruhr led to a vast, reckless printing of paper notes with the deliberate object of destroying the whole basis of the currency. In the final stages of the inflation the Mark stood at forty-three million millions to the pound sterling. The social and economic consequences of this inflation were deadly and far-reaching. The savings of the middle classes were wiped out, and a natural following was thus provided for the banners of National Socialism. The whole structure of German industry was distorted by the growth of mushroom trusts. The entire working capital of the country disappeared. The internal national debt and the debt of industry in the form of fixed capital charges and mortgages were of course simultaneously liquidated or repudiated. But this was no compensation for the loss of working capital. All led directly to the large-scale borrowings of a bankrupt nation abroad which were the feature of ensuing years. German sufferings and bitterness marched forward together—as they do to-day.

The British temper towards Germany, which at first had been so fierce, very soon went as far astray in the opposite direction. A rift opened between Lloyd George and Poincaré, whose bristling personality hampered his firm and far-sighted policies. The two nations fell apart in thought and action, and British sympathy or even admiration for Germany found powerful expression.

## American Disinterest

The League of Nations had no sooner been created than it received an almost mortal blow. The United States abandoned President Wilson's offspring. The President himself, ready to do battle for his ideals, suffered a paralytic stroke just as he was setting forth on his campaign, and lingered henceforward a futile wreck for a great part of two long and vital years, at the end of which his Party and his policy were swept away by the Republican Presidential victory of 1920. Across the Atlantic on the morrow of the Republican success isolationist conceptions prevailed. Europe must be left to stew in its own juice, and must pay its lawful debts. At the same time tariffs were raised to prevent the entry of the goods by which alone these debts could be discharged. At the Washington Conference of 1921, far-reaching proposals for naval disarmament were made by the United States, and the British and American Governments proceeded to sink their battleships and break up their military establishments with gusto. It was argued in odd logic that it would be immoral to disarm the vanquished unless the victors also stripped themselves of their weapons. The finger of Anglo-American reprobation was presently to be pointed at France, deprived alike of the Rhine frontier and of her treaty guarantee, for maintaining, even on a greatly reduced scale, a French Army based upon universal service.

The United States made it clear to Britain that the continuance of her alliance with Japan, to which the Japanese had punctiliously conformed, would constitute a barrier in Anglo-American relations. Accordingly this alliance was brought to an end. The annulment caused a profound impression in Japan, and was viewed as the spurning of an Asiatic Power by the Western World. Many links were sundered which might afterwards have proved of decisive value to peace. At the same time, Japan could console herself with the fact that the downfall of Germany and Russia had, for a time, raised her to the third place among the world's naval Powers, and certainly to the highest rank. Although the Washington Naval Agreement prescribed a lower ratio of strength in capital ships for Japan than for Britain and the United States (five: five: three), the quota assigned to her was well up to her building and financial capacity for a good many years, and she watched with an attentive eye the two leading naval Powers cutting each other down far below what their resources would have permitted and what their responsibilities enjoined. Thus, both in Europe and in Asia, conditions were swiftly created by the victorious Allies which, in the name of peace, cleared the way for the renewal of war.

While all these untoward events were taking place, amid a ceaseless chatter of well-meant platitudes on both sides of the Atlantic, a new and more terrible cause of quarrel than the Imperialism of Czars and Kaisers became apparent in Europe. The Civil War in Russia ended in the absolute victory of the Bolshevik Revolution. The Soviet Armies which advanced to subjugate Poland were indeed repulsed in the battle of Warsaw, but Germany and Italy nearly succumbed to Communist propaganda and designs, and Hungary actually fell for a while under the control of the Communist dictator, Bela Kun. Although Marshal Foch wisely observed that "Bolshevism had never crossed the frontiers of victory", the foundations of European civilisation trembled in the early post-war years. Fascism was the shadow or ugly child of Communism. While Corporal Hitler was making himself useful to the German officer-class in Munich by arousing soldiers and workers to fierce hatred of Jews and Communists, on whom he laid the blame of Germany's defeat, another adventurer, Benito Mussolini, provided Italy with a new theme of government which, while it claimed to save the Italian people from Communism, raised himself to dictatorial power. As Fascism sprang from Communism, so Nazism developed from Fascism. Thus were set on foot those kindred movements which were destined soon to plunge the world into even more hideous strife, which none can say has ended with their destruction.

Nevertheless one solid security for peace remained. Germany was disarmed. All her artillery and weapons were destroyed. Her fleet had already sunk itself in Scapa Flow.

Her vast army was disbanded. By the Treaty of Versailles only a professional long-service army, not exceeding one hundred thousand men, and unable on this basis to accumulate reserves, was permitted to Germany for purposes of internal order. The annual quotas of recruits no longer received their training; the cadres were dissolved. Every effort was made to reduce to a tithe the officer Corps. No military air force of any kind was allowed. Submarines were forbidden, and the German Navy was limited to a handful of vessels under 10,000 tons. Soviet Russia was barred off from Western Europe by a cordon of violently anti-Bolshevik States, who had broken away from the former Empire of the Czars in its new and more terrible form. Poland and Czechoslovakia raised independent heads, and seemed to stand erect in Central Europe. Hungary had recovered from her dose of Bela Kun. The French Army, resting upon its laurels, was incomparably the strongest military force in Europe, and it was for some years believed that the French Air Force was also of a high order.

Up till the year 1934 the power of the conquerors remained unchallenged in Europe and indeed throughout the world. There was no moment in these sixteen years when the three former Allies, or even Britain and France with their associates in Europe, could not in the name of the League of Nations and under its moral and international shield have controlled by a mere effort of the will the armed strength of Germany. Instead, until 1931 the victors and particularly the United States concentrated their efforts upon extorting by vexatious foreign controls their annual reparations from Germany. The fact that these payments were made only from far larger American loans reduced the whole process to the absurd. Nothing was reaped except ill-will. On the other hand, the strict enforcement at any time till 1934 of the Disarmament Clauses of the Peace Treaty would have guarded indefinitely, without violence or bloodshed, the peace and safety of mankind. But this was neglected while the infringements remained petty, and shunned as they assumed serious proportions. Thus the final safeguard of a long peace was cast away. The crimes of the vanquished find their background and their explanation, though not, of course, their pardon, in the follies of the victors. Without these follies crime would have found neither temptation nor opportunity.

# 2

# The Treaty Dooms Germany to Poverty and Starvation

John Maynard Keynes

John Maynard Keynes, one of the most influential economists of the twentieth century, served as a British representative to the Paris Peace Conference. In the following passage from his 1920 book *The Economic Consequences of the Peace*, Keynes argues that the Treaty of Versailles will cause untold economic misery to Germany. As an industrialized nation, Keynes notes, Germany had come to rely on its overseas colonies for jobs and for natural resources, and could not hope to feed itself adequately if those were taken away. Moreover, the reparations Germany was required to pay would burden the country further. Due to declines in such areas as coal production and transportation, Keynes adds, all of Europe as well as Germany would be subject to shortages. The result will be continued political and social instability.

---

This chapter must be one of pessimism. The Treaty includes no provisions for the economic rehabilitation of Europe,—nothing to make the defeated Central Empires into good neighbors, nothing to stabilize the new States of Europe, nothing to reclaim Russia; nor does it promote in any way a compact of economic solidarity amongst the Allies themselves; no arrangement was reached at Paris for restoring the disordered finances of France and Italy, or to adjust the systems of the Old World and the New.

Excerpted from *The Economic Consequences of the Peace* (New York: Harcourt, 1920) by John Maynard Keynes.

## The Allies Ignored Economic Circumstances

The Council of Four paid no attention to these issues, being preoccupied with others,—Clemenceau to crush the economic life of his enemy, Lloyd George to do a deal and bring home something which would pass muster for a week, the President to do nothing that was not just and right. It is an extraordinary fact that the fundamental economic problems of a Europe starving and disintegrating before their eyes, was the one question in which it was impossible to arouse the interest of the Four. Reparation was their main excursion into the economic field, and they settled it as a problem of theology, of politics, of electoral chicane, from every point of view except that of the economic future of the States whose destiny they were handling.

I leave, from this point onwards, Paris, the Conference, and the Treaty, briefly to consider the present situation of Europe, as the War and the Peace have made it; and it will no longer be part of my purpose to distinguish between the inevitable fruits of the War and the avoidable misfortunes of the Peace.

---

*In a very short time . . . Germany will not be in a position to give bread and work to her numerous millions of inhabitants, who are prevented from earning their livelihood by navigation and trade.*

---

The essential facts of the situation, as I see them, are expressed simply. Europe consists of the densest aggregation of population in the history of the world. This population is accustomed to a relatively high standard of life, in which, even now, some sections of it anticipate improvement rather than deterioration. In relation to other continents Europe is not self-sufficient; in particular it cannot feed itself. Internally the population is not evenly distributed, but much of it is crowded into a relatively small number of dense industrial centers. This population secured for itself a livelihood before the war, without much margin of surplus, by means of a delicate and immensely complicated organization, of which the foundations were supported by coal, iron, transport, and an unbroken supply of imported food and raw materials from other continents. By the destruction of this organization and the interruption of the stream of supplies, a part of this population is deprived of its means of livelihood. Emigration is not open to the redundant surplus. For it would take years to transport them overseas, even, which is not the case, if countries could be found which were ready to receive them. The danger confronting us, therefore, is the rapid depression of the standard of life of the European populations to a point which will mean actual starvation for some (a point already reached in Russia and approximately reached in Austria). Men will not always die quietly. For starvation, which brings to some lethargy and a helpless despair, drives other temperaments to the nervous instability of hysteria and to a mad despair. And these in their distress may overturn the remnants of organization, and submerge civilization itself in their attempts to satisfy desperately the overwhelming needs of the individual. This is the danger against which all our resources and courage and idealism must now co-operate.

## Economic Disaster for Germany

On the 13th May, 1919, Count Brockdorff-Rantzau addressed to the Peace Conference of the Allied and Associated Powers the Report of the German Economic Commission charged with the study of the effect of the conditions of Peace on the situation of the German population. "In the course of the last two generations," they reported, "Germany has become transformed from an agricultural State to an industrial State. So long as she was an agricultural State, Germany could feed forty million inhabitants. As an industrial State she could insure the means of subsistence for a population of sixty-seven millions; and in 1913 the importation of foodstuffs amounted, in round figures, to twelve million tons. Before the war a total of fifteen million persons in Germany provided for their existence by foreign trade, navigation, and the use, directly or indirectly, of foreign raw material." After rehearsing the main relevant provisions of the Peace Treaty the report continues: "After this diminution of her products, after the economic depression resulting from the loss of her colonies, her merchant fleet and her foreign investments, Germany will not be in a position to import from abroad an adequate quantity of raw material. An enormous part of German industry will, therefore, be condemned inevitably to destruction. The need of importing foodstuffs will increase considerably at the same time that the possibility of satisfying this demand is as greatly diminished. In a very short time, therefore, Germany will not be in a position to give bread and work to her numerous millions of inhabitants, who are prevented from earning their livelihood by navigation and trade. These persons should emigrate, but this is a material impossibility, all the more because many countries and the most important ones will oppose any German immigration. To put the Peace conditions into execution would logically involve, therefore, the loss of several millions of persons in Germany. This catastrophe would not be long in coming about, seeing that the health of the population has been broken down during the War by the Blockade, and during the Armistice by the aggravation of the Blockade of famine. No help, however great, or over however long a period it were continued, could prevent these deaths *en masse.*" "We do not know, and indeed we doubt," the report concludes, "whether the Delegates of the Allied and Associated Powers realize the inevitable consequences which will take place if Germany, an industrial State, very thickly populated, closely bound up with the economic system of the world, and under the necessity of importing enormous quantities of raw material and foodstuffs, suddenly finds herself pushed back to the phase of her development, which corresponds to her economic condition and the numbers of her population as they were half a century ago. Those who sign this Treaty will sign the death sentence of many millions of German men, women and children."

---

*"Those who sign this Treaty will sign the death sentence of many millions of German men, women and children."*

---

I know of no adequate answer to these words. The indictment is at least as true of the Austrian, as of the German, settlement. This is the fundamental problem in front of us, before which questions of territorial adjustment and the balance of European power are insignificant. Some of the catastrophes of past history, which have thrown back human progress for centuries, have been due to the reactions following on the sudden termination, whether in the course of nature or by the act of man, of temporarily favorable conditions which have permitted the growth of population beyond what could be provided for when the favorable conditions were at an end.

## Central Europe's Poverty and Disorder

The significant features of the immediate situation can be grouped under three heads: first, the absolute falling off, for the time being, in Europe's internal productivity; second, the breakdown of transport and exchange by means of which its products could be conveyed where they were most wanted; and third, the inability of Europe to purchase its usual supplies from overseas.

The decrease of productivity cannot be easily estimated, and may be the subject of exaggeration. But the *primâ facie* evidence of it is overwhelming, and this factor has been the main burden of Mr. Hoover's well-considered warnings [future U.S. President Herbert Hoover was head of an American relief mission in Postwar Europe]. A variety of causes have produced it;—violent and prolonged internal disorder as in Russia and Hungary; the creation of new governments and their inexperience in the readjustment of economic relations, as in Poland and Czecho-Slovakia; the loss throughout the Continent of efficient labor, through the casualties of war or the continuance of mobilization; the falling-off in efficiency through continued underfeeding in the Central Empires; the exhaustion of the soil from lack of the usual applications of artificial manures throughout the course of the war; the unsettlement of the minds of the laboring classes on the above all (to quote Mr. Hoover), "there is a great fundamental economic issue of their lives. But relaxation of effort as the reflex of physical exhaustion of large sections of the population from privation and the mental and physical strain of the war." Many persons are for one reason or another out of employment altogether. According to Mr. Hoover, a summary of the unemployment bureas in Europe in July, 1919, showed that 15,000,000 families were receiving unemployment allowances in one form or another, and were being paid in the main by a constant inflation of currency. In Germany there is the added deterrent to labor and to capital (in so far as the Reparation terms are

taken literally), that anything, which they may produce beyond the barest level of subsistence, will for years to come
be taken away from them.

Such definite data as we possess do not add much, perhaps, to the general picture of decay. But I will remind the
reader of one or two of them. The coal production of Europe as a whole is estimated to have fallen off by 30 per cent;
and upon coal the greater part of the industries of Europe
and the whole of her transport system depend. Whereas before the war Germany produced 85 per cent of the total food
consumed by her inhabitants, the productivity of the soil is
now diminished by 40 per cent and the effective quality of
the live-stock by 55 per cent. Of the European countries
which formerly possessed a large exportable surplus, Russia,
as much by reason of deficient transport as of diminished
output, may herself starve. Hungary, apart from her other
troubles, has been pillaged by the Roumanians immediately
after harvest. Austria will have consumed the whole of her
own harvest for 1919 before the end of the calendar year.
The figures are almost too overwhelming to carry conviction
to our minds; if they were not quite so bad, our effective belief in them might be stronger.

But even when coal can be got and grain harvested, the
breakdown of the European railway system prevents their
carriage; and even when goods can be manufactured, the
breakdown of the European currency system prevents their
sale. I have already described the losses, by war and under the
Armistice surrenders, to the transport system of Germany.
But even so, Germany's position, taking account of her
power of replacement by manufacture, is probably not so serious as that of some of her neighbors. In Russia (about
which, however, we have very little exact or accurate information) the condition of the rolling-stock is believed to be altogether desperate, and one of the most fundamental factors
in her existing economic disorder. And in Poland, Roumania,
and Hungary the position is not much better. Yet modern industrial life essentially depends on efficient transport facili-
ties, and the population which secured its livelihood by these
means cannot continue to live without them. The breakdown
of currency, and the distrust in its purchasing value, is an aggravation of these evils which must be discussed in a little
more detail in connection with foreign trade.

What then is our picture of Europe? A country population able to support life on the fruits of its own agricultural production but without the accustomed surplus for the towns, and also (as a result of the lack of imported materials and so of variety and amount in the saleable manufactures of the towns) without the usual incentives to market food in return for other wares; an industrial population unable to keep its strength for lack of food, unable to earn a livelihood for lack of materials, and so unable to make good by imports from abroad the failure of productivity at home.

# 3

# Critics Ignored the Positive Aspects of the Treaty

David Lloyd George

David Lloyd George, Prime Minister of Great Britain from 1916 to 1922 and one of the architects of the Treaty of Versailles, seeks to defend the treaty from its many critics in the following passage, written in 1923. Lloyd George, using a measure of irony and sarcasm, claims that few critics actually read the treaty and simply complained about it according to their various points of view. Others ignored the freedoms established by the treaty's territorial changes. Still others failed to recognize that the covenant of the League of Nations, the first truly international diplomatic body and the precursor to the United Nations, was contained in the treaty.

---

I have had recently special opportunities for appreciating the extent to which the Treaty of Versailles has not been read by those who have formed very definite opinions concerning its qualities. There is no justification for a failure to peruse this great international instrument. It is the most important document of modern times. It has reshaped for better or for worse much of the geography of Europe. It has resurrected dead and buries nationalities. It constitutes the deed of manumission of tens of millions of Europeans who, up to the year of victory, 1918, were the bondsmen of other races. It affects profoundly the economics, the finance, the industrial and trade conditions of the world; it contains

Excerpted from *Where Are We Going?* by David Lloyd George (New York: George H. Doran, 1923).

clauses upon the efficacy of which may depend the very existence of our civilisation. Nevertheless there are few who can tell you what is in the Treaty of Versailles. You might have thought that although men differed widely as to its merits, there would have been no difficulty in securing some measure of agreement as to its actual contents. Every endeavour was made to give full publicity to the draft when it was first presented to the Germans, and to the final document when signed. Even before the form of the draft was ever settled, the actual decisions were reported from day to day. Never was a treaty so reported and so discussed in every article and every particle of its constitution, and to-day you can procure an official copy of it from any bookseller for the moderate price of 2*s*. 6*d*. In spite of that no two men who happen to profess diverse opinions as to its justice or injustice can agree as to its contents.

A visitor to England in the year 1713 probably experienced the same perplexity in seeking information from a Whig and a Tory respectively as to the Treaty of Utrecht. So this treaty has become one of those fiercely debated subjects, as to which the contestants deliberately refuse to regard any testimony, or recognise the existence of any fact, which is in the least inconsistent with their particular point of view. It has come to pass that the real Treaty of Versailles has already disappeared, and several imaginary versions have emerged. It is around these that the conflict rages.

## Interpretations of the Treaty

In France there exist at least two or three schools of thought concerning the Versailles Treaty. There is one powerful section which has always regarded it as a treasonable pact, in which M. Clemenceau gave away solid French rights and interests in a moment of weakness under pressure from President Wilson and myself. That is the Poincaré-Barthou-Pertinax school. That is why they are now, whilst in form engaged in enforcing the treaty, in fact carrying out a gigantic operation for amending it without consulting the other signatories. This has come out very clearly in the remarkable report from a French official in the Rhineland which was disclosed in the London *Observer*. It is obvious from this paper that whilst the French government have worked their public into a frenzied state of indignation over the failure of Germany to carry out the Treaty of Versailles, they were the whole time deliberately organising a plot to overthrow that treaty themselves. Their representative on the Rhine was spending French money with the consent of the French government to promote a conspiracy for setting up an independent republic on the Rhine under the protection of France. It was a deliberate attempt by those who disapproved of the moderation of the Treaty of Versailles to rewrite its clauses in the terms of the militarist demands put forward by Marshal Foch at the Peace conference. Marshal Foch, the soul of honour, wanted to see this done openly and straightforwardly. What he would have done like the gentleman he is, these conspirators would have accomplished by deceit—by deceiving their Allies and by being faithless to the treaty to which their country had appended its signature. That is one French school of thought on the Treaty of Versailles. It is the one which has brought Europe to its present state of confusion and despair.

---

*It has come to pass that the real Treaty of Versailles has already disappeared, and several imaginary versions have emerged.*

---

There is the second school which reads into the treaty powers and provisions which it does not contain, and never contemplated containing. These critics maintain stoutly that M. Briand, and all other French prime ministers, with the exception of M. Poincaré, betrayed their trust by failing to enforce these imaginary stipulations. They still honestly believe that M. Poincaré is the first French minister to have made a genuine attempt to enforce French rights under the treaty.

In the background there is a third school which knows exactly what the treaty means, but dares not say so in the present state of French opinion. Perhaps they think it is better to bide their time. That time will come, and when it does arrive, let us hope it will not be too late to save Europe from the welter.

## Differing American Opinions

In America there are also two or three divergent trends of opinion about this treaty. One regards it as an insidious attempt to trap America into the European cockpit, so as to pluck its feathers to line French and English bolsters. If anything could justify so insular an estimate it would be the entirely selfish interpretation which is put upon the treaty by one or two of the Allied governments. The other American party, I understand, defends it with vigour as a great human instrument second only in importance to the Declaration of Independence. There may be a third which thinks that on the whole it is not a bad settlement, and that the pity is a little more tact was not displayed in passing it through the various stages of approval and ratification. This party is not as vocal as the others.

---

*The covenant of the League of Nations is lifted bodily out of the text, and is delivered to the public as a separate testament for the faithful so that the saints may not defile their hands with the polluted print which exacts justice.*

---

In England we find at least three schools. There are the critics who denounce it as a brutal outrage upon international justice. It is to them a device for extorting incalculable sums out of an impoverished Germany as reparation for damages artificially worked up. Then there is the other extreme—the "die-hard" section—more influential since it became less numerous, who think the treaty let Germany off much too lightly. In fact they are in complete agreement with the French Chauvinists as to the reprehensible moderation of its terms. In Britain also there is a third party which regards its provisions as constituting the best settlement, when you take into account the conflicting aims, interests, and traditions of the parties who had to negotiate and come to an agreement.

## Critics Ignored the League of Nations Covenant

But take all these variegated schools together, or separately, and you will find not one in a thousand of their pupils could give you an intelligent and comprehensive summary of the main principles of the treaty. I doubt whether I should be far wrong in saying there would not be one in ten thousand. Controversialists generally are satisfied to concentrate on the articles in the treaty which are obnoxious or pleasing to them as the case may be, and ignore the rest completely, however essential they may be to a true judgment of the whole. Most of the disputants are content to take their views from press comments and denunciatory speeches. Unhappily the explanatory speeches have been few. Some there are who have in their possession the full text—nominally for reference; but you will find parts of the reparations clauses in their copies black with the thumb-marks which note the perspiring dialectician searching for projectiles to hurl at the object of his fury. The clauses which ease and modify the full demand are treated with stern neglect, and the remainder of the pages are pure as the untrodden snow. You can trace no footprints of politicians, publicists, or journalists, in whole provinces of this unexplored treaty. The covenant of the League of Nations is lifted bodily out of the text, and is delivered to the public as a separate testament for the faithful so that the saints may not defile their hands with the polluted print which exacts justice. They have now come to believe that it never was incorporated in the Treaty of Versailles, and that it has nothing to do with that vile and sanguinary instrument.

And yet the first words of this treaty are the following:

"The High Contracting Parties,

"In order to promote international co-operation and to achieve international peace and security

"By the acceptance of obligations not to resort to war,

"By the prescription of open, just and honourable relations between nations,

"By the firm establishment of the understandings of international law as the actual rule of conduct among Governments, and

"By the maintenance of justice and a scrupulous respect for all treaty obligations in the dealings of organised peoples with one another,

"Agree to this Covenant of the League of Nations."

Then follow the articles of the debated covenant.

A speaker who took part recently in a university debate on the subject told me that the undergraduates exhibited the greatest surprise when he informed them that the League of Nations was founded by the Versailles Treaty. A few days ago I had a similar experience at the Oxford Union. I was speaking against a motion framed to condemn the principles of the treaty as unwise and unjust. In its defence I recalled some of its outstanding features. But as most of my narrative had no bearing on reparations it was greeted with impatience and cries of "Question" from a group of anti-Versaillists. They honestly thought I was travelling outside the motion in giving a short summary of the other sections of the treaty. To them it is all condensed in Mr. Keynes's book [*The Economic Consequences of the Peace*, by John Maynard Keynes], and other hostile commentaries. Anything which is inconsistent with these, or supplements the scanty or misleading statements they make, is deemed to be tainted and biassed. To refer to the text itself they regard as unfair, and as playing into the hands of the defenders of a wicked and oppressive pact. The actual treaty has been already put by them out of bounds, and you wander into its forbidden clauses on pain of being put into the guardroom by one or other of the intolerant factions who patrol the highways and byways of international politics.

In all the debates on the subject in the House of Commons I have only once heard the treaty itself quoted by a critic, and strangely enough that was by way of approval.

I have indicated one important section of the treaty to which is accorded something of the reverence due to Holy Writ by an influential section of the public. This group would be shocked were they reminded that their devotion is given to a chapter in the hateful treaty. There is yet another large and important section which is completely ignored by the critics—that which reconstructs Central Europe on the basis of nationality and the free choice of the people instead of on the basis of strategy and military convenience. This is the section that liberated Poland from the claws of the three carnivorous empires that were preying on its vitals, and restored it to life, liberty and independence. It is the section that frees the Danes of Schleswig and the Frenchmen of Alsace-Lorraine. For these oppressed provinces the Treaty of Versailles is the title-deed of freedom. Why are these clauses all suppressed in controversial literature?

# 4

# Great Britain, France, and the United States Failed to Support the Treaty

Michael L. Dockrill and J. Douglas Goold

In the following passage, Michael L. Dockrill and J. Douglas Goold suggest that the failure of the Treaty of Versailles lay in the unwillingness of the Allied powers to uphold it. The United States Senate rejected it entirely, which meant that the United States also decided against participation in the League of Nations. Britain, in turn lost faith in both the League and in the treaty, while other disagreements soured the Anglo-French relationship. The treaty was approved partly, the authors suggest, to mitigate strong anti-German sentiment among the Allied publics immediately after World War I, and leaders hoped that over time some of its harsher provisions might be changed, but even that effort failed.

Michael L. Dockrill is professor of history at Oxford University. J. Douglas Goold is professor of history at the University of Edmonton in Alberta, Canada.

---

The most serious blow to British calculations about the future was the American Senate's rejection of the Treaty of Versailles. Since, on Wilson's insistence, the Covenant of the League of Nations was incorporated in that treaty, the League had to start its life without the participation of the United States. Lloyd George had always been lukewarm about the League but, as Woodrow Wilson had placed that organization at the forefront of his vision for the future, and as future British policy was to be based on Anglo-American cooperation, the Prime Minister was compelled to support the League during the conference. If American enthusiasm for the League waned during 1919, that of the British public did not, if demonstrations in its favour, such as the mass rally of the League of Nations Union at the Mansion House on 13 October 1919, were any indication. In the words of a recent historian of the League, 'with a good press and powerful backing from the churches, the League enjoyed a public support that the government could not afford to disappoint'.

Nevertheless the British Government made it clear that it was not prepared to abandon any of its historic safeguards for the sake of the flimsy and dubious protection offered by the League organization. In a June 1919 White Paper the Government insisted that the best protection against aggression was 'the public opinon of the civilized world'. Since this was the only sanction on which Britain was prepared to base the League system, it was obvious that she intended to maintain her future security on the traditional instruments of the balance of power, the British Empire and British naval strength.

British leaders regarded a League which included the United States as a shaky enough enterprise, likely to be held together only by continued cooperation between the two powers. A League without the United States was regarded with acute misgivings. In order to maintain close relations with Wilson and to coordinate Anglo-American policy over naval relations, Ireland and the League, the British government sent Lord Grey of Fallodon, the former foreign secretary and a president of the League of Nations Union, on a special mission to the United States in September. This mission was a complete failure. Grey never even saw the ailing President. By the end of 1919 it was clear that the American Senate would never ratify the Treaty of Versailles.

## America Turns Away from International Involvement

Lloyd George and his supporters could see little future in a League of Nations without the United States. On 5 November Cecil Hurst, the foreign office legal expert, lunched with Hankey, Kerr, Balfour and Drummond and reported to Hardinge that 'the view was expressed very strongly by Mr Kerr and Sir Maurice Hankey that the League of Nations could not really exist if the United States was not a member and I think Mr Balfour is inclined to agree'. Lloyd George certainly agreed, but was compelled by popular opinion to support the League, at least in public. In part because of British doubts and hesitations about the League, it was to fulfil none of the hopes of its originators. And with the failure of the United States to ratify the Versailles Treaty, the main plank in Britain's postwar plans, close and cordial relations between Britain and the United States, collapsed.

---

*Both Woodrow Wilson and Lloyd George shared the assumption that the aggressor must make amends for his wrong-doing, and their attitudes corresponded to that (those) of broad cross-sections of allied public opinion.*

---

In the same period American participation in the shaping of post-war Europe virtually ceased. Frank Polk remained as the American delegate to the Peace Conference after Lansing had departed in August. Polk could seldom secure coherent instructions from Washington and so Britain and France were left, with haphazard support from Italy, to resolve the remaining issues without either American interference or support. After December 1919, when the conference was dissolved, and executive powers were transferred to the conference of ambassadors in Paris, the American ambassador attended its meetings only as an observer. The lingering hopes of the defeated nations that the United States would mitigate the harsher aspects of the settlements vanished.

For many in Britain the aftermath of the Treaty of Versailles was one of disillusionment and despair. This was fuelled by the outspoken attacks on the treaty by Keynes and other intellectuals, who represented the settlement as a betrayal of the promises made by Woodrow Wilson during the war. Repeated German protests about the harsh nature of the treaty kept the issue alive during the 1920s and beyond. In fact, from the point of view of her national interests, Britain had not done badly out of the post-war settlement. The German fleet no longer presented any threat to Great Britain while Germany's colonies were, for the most part, controlled by Britain and her empire. She had secured at least a promise of a share in whatever reparations could be extracted from Germany. Germany had also been confined to reduced boundaries.

## Britain and France Disagree over the Treatment of Germany

Lloyd George and his associates could at least congratulate themselves on having protected Germany from the more extreme demands of the French, and had even secured last minute adjustments in the treaty in Germany's favour. However the British Government also believed that Germany, by her conduct during and after 1914, justly deserved all the other impositions of the treaty. Punishment was a central motif in Britain's policy towards the defeated nations. While right-wing *enragés* like Hardinge insisted that 'the big stick is what bullies like them [the Germans] understand better than anything else', a recent writer has commented that 'the punitive overtones of the moralism of the moderate left have to be taken seriously'. Both Woodrow Wilson and Lloyd George shared the assumption that the aggressor must make amends for his wrong-doing, and their attitudes corresponded to that of broad cross-sections of allied public opinion.

Woodrow Wilson hoped that the harsher aspects of the treaties could be mitigated later by the League of Nations, which was presumably to engage in a continuous process of treaty revision. His faith in the future efficacy of the League must explain his almost cavalier attitude towards some of the more outrageous treaty provisions, despite Lloyd George's frequent reminders that Wilson's own principles were at stake. Lloyd George hoped that Germany would, after initial protests, settle down within her new frontiers and concentrate on economic reconstruction. When she showed no signs of doing so, he began to champion a more conciliatory approach. The French had every reason to be irritated by Britain's behaviour. At Paris Britain had led the way in insisting on a very high level of reparations. Later,

however, she gave little or no support to French efforts to
extract them. Britain used America's rejection of the guarantee to France as an opportunity to renounce her part of
the pact. She had played a leading role in the peace settlements, but showed no inclination to assist France in up-
holding them.

The British argued, with some justice, that foreign policy must evolve in the light of changing circumstances. After a short term post-war boom, unemployment in Britain
climbed to relatively high levels. Lloyd George began to
search for a long term recovery of Britain's trade which, in
turn, seemed to depend on the recovery of German (and
Russian) economic life. French insistence on the extraction
of large sums from Germany threatened the success of his
plans, as well as keeping alive German resentment about the
treaty. By 1921 post-war passions in Britain had subsided;
those in France had not.

---

*It was not the Treaty that was at the root of the*
*problems of the inter-war period. It was the*
*inability of France and Britain, the two great*
*powers with most at stake in the settlement,*
*either to agree to uphold the Treaty or to find*
*some means of alleviating it.*

---

Franco-British differences widened after the ratification
of the Treaty of Versailles on 10 January 1920. Woodrow
Wilson's miscalculations resulted in the withdrawal of the
United States from active participation in post-war European policies, while increasing Anglo-French disputes destroyed the possibility of meaningful cooperation between
them. France, deprived of the Anglo-American guarantee,
adopted an intransigent attitude towards every German in-
fringement of the Versailles Treaty. Of course the lines of
French post-war policy were by no means clearly defined in
1920. Nor did Britain exhibit much consistency in her approach to European questions, but the beginnings of a more
conciliatory approach towards Germany and Bolshevik
Russia were already becoming evident.

Both Britain and France were more or less able to
thwart the other's German policies but were unable individ-

ually to impose a coherent long term unilateral solution. It was not the Treaty that was at the root of the problems of the inter-war period. It was the inability of France and Britain, the two great powers with most at stake in the settlement, either to agree to uphold the Treaty or to find some means of alleviating it.

# 5

# Adolf Hitler Denounces the Treaty of Versailles

Adolf Hitler

From the period when he emerged as a rabble rouser in post–World War I Munich until World War II, Nazi dictator Adolf Hitler railed against the Treaty of Versailles. Indeed, Hitler's call to rescind the treaty became both a rallying cry and a practical goal; not only did he constantly urge Germans to agitate against the treaty, he actively defied it after achieving power in 1933 by building up Germany's armed forces beyond the levels stipulated at Versailles. Hitler saw the treaty as a grave insult to Germans and claimed that the Weimar Republic, which had approved it, had stabbed Germany in the back.

In the following speech, made in 1939, Hitler claims that the greatest of the crimes of Versailles was its destruction of Germany's territorial boundaries. Germans, he asserts, were denied the territorial integrity granted to other nations. Not only was this an insult, it ignored, as Hitler saw it, the truth of one thousand years of German history and culture. He believed it was his destiny to repudiate the treaty and restore Germany's "true" boundaries.

---

**"S**ince the day on which I entered politics I have been moved by no other idea than that of winning back the freedom of the German nation, restoring the power and strength of the Reich, overcoming the internal disruption of the nation, remedying its isolation from the rest of the world, and safeguarding the maintenance of its independent economic and political existence."

Excerpted from Adolf Hitler's speech as it appeared in *The Speeches of Adolf Hitler, April 1922–August 1939*, vol. 2, edited by Norman H. Baynes (Oxford: Oxford University Press, under the auspices of the Royal Institute of International Affairs, 1942).

"I have worked only to restore that which others once broke by force, I have desired only to make good that which Satanic malice or human unreason destroyed or demolished. I have therefore taken no step which violated the rights of others, but have only restored that justice which was violated twenty years ago. The present Greater German Reich contains no territory which was not from the earliest times a part of this Reich, not bound up with it or subject to its sovereignty. Long before an American Continent had been discovered—to say nothing of settled—by white people, this Reich existed, not merely in its present extent, but with the addition of many regions and provinces which have since been lost."

"One of the most shameful acts of oppression ever committed is the dismemberment of the German nation and the political disintegration of her living space—which has, after all, been hers for thousands of years—provided for in the Dictate of Versailles."

---

*"One of the most shameful acts of oppression ever committed is the dismemberment of the German nation and the political disintegration of her living space—which has, after all, been hers for thousands of years—provided for in the Dictate of Versailles."*

---

"I have never, Gentlemen, left any doubt that in point of fact it is scarcely possible anywhere in Europe to arrive at a harmony of State and national boundaries which will be satisfactory in every way. On the one hand the migration of peoples which gradually came to a standstill during the last few centuries, and the development of large communities on the other have brought about a situation which, whatever way they look at it, must necessarily be considered unsatisfactory by those concerned. It was, however, the very way in which these national and political developments were gradually stabilized in the last century which led many to consider themselves justified in cherishing the hope that in the end a compromise would be found between respect for the national life of the various European peoples and the recognition of established political structures—a compromise by which, without destroying the political order in Europe and with it the existing economic basis, nationalities could nevertheless be preserved. This hope was abolished by the Great War. The Peace-Dictate of Versailles did justice neither to the one principle nor to the other. Neither the right of self-determination nor yet the political, let alone the economic, necessities and conditions for the European development were respected. Nevertheless I never left any doubt that—as I have already emphasized—even a revision of the Treaty of Versailles would also find its limit somewhere. And I have always said so with the utmost frankness—not for any tactical reasons but from my innermost conviction.

## Germany Was Not the Cause of International Tensions

As the national leader of the German people I have never left any doubt that, wherever the higher interests of the European comity were at stake, national interests must, if necessary, be relegated to second place in certain cases. And—as I have already emphasized—this is not for tactical reasons; for I have never left any doubt that I am absolutely earnest in this attitude of mine. For quite a number of territories which might possibly be disputed I have therefore come to final decisions which I have proclaimed not only to the outside world, but also to my own people, and have seen to it that they should abide by them." "I have never changed my attitude nor will I ever do so. . . . The return of the Saar territory has done away with all territorial problems in Europe between France and Germany. . . . I have confirmed this attitude to France as an expression of an appreciation of the necessity to attain peace in Europe instead of sowing the seed of continual uncertainty and even tension by making unlimited demands and continually asking for revision. If this tension has nevertheless now arisen, the responsibility does not lie with Germany, but with those international elements which systematically produce such tension in order to serve their capitalist interests."

"I have given binding declarations to a large number of States. None of these States can complain that even a trace of a demand contrary thereto has ever been made to them by Germany. None of the Scandinavian statesmen, for example, can contend that a request has ever been put to them by the German Government or by German public opinion which was incompatible with the sovereignty and integrity of their State."

"I was pleased that a number of European States availed themselves of these declarations by the German Government to express and emphasize their desire too for absolute neutrality. This applies to Holland, Belgium, Switzerland, Denmark, &c. I have already mentioned France. I need not mention Italy, with whom we are united in the deepest and closest friendship, Hungary and Yugoslavia, with whom we as neighbours have the fortune to be on very friendly terms. On the other hand I have left no doubt from the first moment of my political activity that there existed other circumstances which represent such a mean and gross outrage of the right of self-determination of our people that we can never accept or endorse them. I have never written a single line or made a single speech displaying a different attitude towards the above-mentioned States. On the other hand with reference to the other cases I have never written a single line or made a single speech in which I have expressed any attitude contrary to my actions."

---

*Not only was the German Reich destroyed and Austria split up into its component parts by the criminals of Versailles, but Germans were also forbidden to acknowledge that community which they had confessed for more than a thousand years.*

---

"I. Austria. The oldest Eastern March of the German people was once the buttress of the German nation on the south-east of the Reich. The Germans of this country are descended from settlers from all the German tribes, even though the Bavarian tribe did contribute the major portion. Later this Ostmark became the crown lands and the nucleus of a five-century-old German Empire, with Vienna as the capital of the German Reich of that period. This German Reich was finally broken up in the course of a gradual dissolution by Napoleon the Corsican but continued to exist as a German Federation, and not so long ago fought and suffered in the greatest war of all time as an entity which was the expression of the national feelings of the people, even if it was no longer one united State. I myself am a child of this Ostmark. Not only was the German Reich destroyed and Austria split up into its component parts by the criminals of Versailles, but Germans were also forbidden to acknowledge that community which they had confessed for more than a thousand years. I have always regarded the elimination of this state of affairs as the highest and most sacred task of my life. I have never failed to proclaim this determination. And I have always been resolved to realize these ideas, which haunted me day and night. I should have sinned against my call by Providence had I failed by my own endeavour to lead my native country and my German people of the Ostmark back to the Reich and thus to the community of the German people."

"In doing so, moreover, I have wiped out the most disgraceful side of the Treaty of Versailles. I have once more established the right of self-determination, and done away with the democratic oppression of seven and a half million Germans. I removed the ban which prevented them from voting on their own fate, and carried out this vote before the whole world. The result was not only what I had expected, but also precisely what had been anticipated by the Versailles democratic oppressors of peoples."

# Chapter 3

# Historical Interpretations of the Treaty

# 1

# Although the Treaty of Versailles Was Reasonable, Few Germans Accepted It

William L. Shirer

In the following excerpt, William L. Shirer argues that Germany was unable to achieve stability after World War I because few Germans accepted either the Treaty of Versailles or the new government of the nation, the Weimar Republic, which they held responsible for submitting to the dictates of the victorious World War I "entente" of Great Britain, France, and the United States. In particular, Shirer asserts, the German army as well as conservatives in industry failed to support the Weimar leaders. Consequently, Germany became a "house divided" while the people suffered from uncertainty, humiliation, and the virtual destruction of the German economy. Nonetheless, Shirer claims that the Treaty of Versailles was not unreasonable, as Germany lost relatively little territory and maintained its integrity as a potentially powerful nation.

Journalist William Shirer lived in and reported on Germany in the 1920s and 1930s and worked as a radio announcer from Europe during World War II.

---

Before the drafting of the Weimar Constitution was finished an inevitable event occurred which cast a spell of doom over it and the Republic which it was to establish. This was the drawing up of the Treaty of Versailles. During the first chaotic and riotous days of the peace and even after the deliberations of the National Assembly got under way in Weimar the German people seemed to give little thought to the consequences of their defeat. Or if they did, they appeared to be smugly confident that having, as the Allies urged, got rid of the Hohenzollerns, squelched the Bolshevists and set about forming a democratic, republican government, they were entitled to a just peace based not on their having lost the war but on President Wilson's celebrated Fourteen Points.

## An Earlier Harsh Treaty

German memories did not appear to stretch back as far as one year, to March 3, 1918, when the then victorious German Supreme Command had imposed on a defeated Russia at Brest Litovsk a peace treaty which to a British historian, writing two decades after the passions of war had cooled, was a "humiliation without precedent or equal in modern history." It deprived Russia of a territory nearly as large as Austria-Hungary and Turkey combined, with 56,000,000 inhabitants, or 32 per cent of her whole population; a third of her railway mileage, 73 per cent of her total iron ore, 89 per cent of her total coal production; and more than 5,000 factories and industrial plants. Moreover, Russia was obliged to pay Germany an indemnity of six billion marks.

The day of reckoning arrived for the Germans in the late spring of 1919. The terms of the Versailles Treaty, laid down by the Allies without negotiation with Germany, were published in Berlin on May 7. They came as a staggering blow to a people who had insisted on deluding themselves to the last moment. Angry mass meetings were organized throughout the country to protest against the treaty and to demand that Germany refuse to sign it. Scheidemann, who had become Chancellor during the Weimar Assembly, cried, "May the hand wither that signs this treaty!" On May 8 Ebert, who had become Provisional President, and the government publicly branded the terms as "unrealizable and unbearable." The next day the German delegation at Versailles wrote the unbending Clemenceau that such a treaty was "intolerable for any nation."

What was so intolerable about it? It restored Alsace-Lorraine to France, a parcel of territory to Belgium, a similar parcel in Schleswig to Denmark—after a plebiscite—

which Bismarck had taken from the Danes in the previous century after defeating them in war. It gave back to the Poles the lands, some of them only after a plebiscite, which the Germans had taken during the partition of Poland. This was one of the stipulations which infuriated the Germans the most, not only because they resented separating East Prussia from the Fatherland by a corridor which gave Poland access to the sea, but because they despised the Poles, whom they considered an inferior race. Scarcely less infuriating to the Germans was that the treaty forced them to accept responsibility for starting the war and demanded that they turn over to the Allies Kaiser Wilhelm II and some eight hundred other "war criminals."

Reparations were to be fixed later, but a first payment of five billion dollars in gold marks was to be paid between 1919 and 1921, and certain deliveries in kind—coal, ships, lumber, cattle, etc.—were to be made in lieu of cash reparations.

But what hurt most was that Versailles virtually disarmed Germany and thus, for the time being anyway, barred the way to German hegemony in Europe. And yet the hated Treaty of Versailles, unlike that which Germany had imposed on Russia, left the Reich geographically and economically largely intact and preserved her political unity and her potential strength as a great nation.

The provisional government at Weimar, with the exception of Erzberger, who urged acceptance of the treaty on the grounds that its terms could be easily evaded, was strongly against accepting the Versailles *Diktat*, as it was now being called. Behind the government stood the overwhelming majority of citizens, from right to left.

And the Army? If the treaty were rejected, could the Army resist an inevitable Allied attack from the west? Ebert put it up to the Supreme Command, which had now moved its headquarters to Kolberg in Pomerania. On June 17 Field Marshal von Hindenburg, prodded by General Groener, who saw that German military resistance would be futile, replied:

> In the event of a resumption of hostilities we can reconquer the province of Posen [in Poland] and defend our frontiers in the east. In the west, however, we can scarcely count upon being able to withstand a serious offensive on the part of the enemy in view of the nu-

merical superiority of the Entente and their ability to outflank us on both wings.

The success of the operation as a whole is therefore very doubtful, but as a soldier I cannot help feeling that it were better to perish honorably than accept a disgraceful peace.

The concluding words of the revered Commander in Chief were in the best German military tradition but their sincerity may be judged by knowledge of the fact which the German people were unaware of—that Hindenburg had agreed with Groener that to try to resist the Allies now would not only be hopeless but might result in the destruction of the cherished officer corps of the Army and indeed of Germany itself.

## An Ultimatum Is Presented

The Allies were now demanding a definite answer from Germany. On June 16, the day previous to Hindenburg's written answer to Ebert, they had given the Germans an ultimatum: Either the treaty must be accepted by June 24 or the armistice agreement would be terminated and the Allied powers would "take such steps as they think necessary to enforce their terms."

Once again Ebert appealed to Groener. If the Supreme Command thought there was the slightest possibility of successful military resistance to the Allies, Ebert promised to try to secure the rejection of the treaty by the Assembly. But he must have an answer immediately. The last day of the ultimatum, June 24, had arrived. The cabinet was meeting at 4:30 P.M. to make its final decision. Once more Hindenburg and Groener conferred. "You know as well as I do that armed resistance is impossible," the aging, worn Field Marshal said. But once again, as at Spa on November 9, 1918, when he could not bring himself to tell the Kaiser the final truth and left the unpleasant duty to Groener, he declined to tell the truth to the Provisional President of the Republic. "You can give the answer to the President as well as I can," he said to Groener. And again the courageous General took the final responsibility which belonged to the Field Marshal, though he must have known that it would eventually make doubly sure his being made a scapegoat for the of-

ficer corps. He telephoned the Supreme Command's view
to the President.

Relieved at having the Army's leaders take the responsibility—a fact that was soon forgotten in Germany—the
National Assembly approved the signing of the peace
treaty by a large majority and its decision was communicated to Clemenceau a bare nineteen minutes before the
Allied ultimatum ran out. Four days later, on June 28, 1919,
the treaty of peace was signed in the Hall of Mirrors in the
Palace of Versailles.

## A House Divided

From that day on Germany became a house divided.

The conservatives would accept neither the treaty of
peace nor the Republic which had ratified it. Nor, in the
long run, would the Army—General Groener excepted—
though it had sworn to support the new democratic regime
and had itself made the final decision to sign at Versailles.
Despite the November "revolution," the conservatives still
held the economic power. They owned the industries, the
large estates and most of the country's capital. Their wealth
could be used, and was, to subsidize political parties and a
political press that would strive from now on to undermine
the Republic.

The Army began to circumvent the military restrictions
of the peace treaty before the ink on it was scarcely dry. And
thanks to the timidity and shortsightedness of the Socialist
leaders, the officer corps managed not only to maintain the
Army in its old Prussian traditions, as we have seen, but to
become the real center of political power in the new Germany. The Army did not, until the last days of the short-
lived Republic, stake its fortunes on any one political move-
ment. But under General Hans von Seeckt, the brilliant
creator of the 100,000-man Reichswehr, the Army, small as
it was in numbers, became a state within a state, exerting an
increasing influence on the nation's foreign and domestic
policies until a point was reached where the Republic's continued existence depended on the will of the officer corps.

As a state within a state it maintained its independence
of the national government. Under the Weimar Constitution the Army could have been subordinated to the cabinet
and Parliament, as the military establishments of the other
Western democracies were. But it was not. Nor was the of-

ficer corps purged of its monarchist, antirepublican frame of mind. A few Socialist leaders such as Scheidemann and Grzesinski urged "democratizing" the armed forces. They saw the danger of handing the Army back to the officers of the old authoritarian, imperialist tradition. But they were successfully opposed not only by the generals but by their fellow Socialists led by the Minister of Defense, Noske. This proletarian minister of the Republic openly boasted that he wanted to revive "the proud soldier memories of the World War." The failure of the duly elected government to build a new Army that would be faithful to its own democratic spirit and subordinate to the cabinet and the Reichstag was a fatal mistake for the Republic, as time would tell.

The failure to clean out the judiciary was another. The administrators of the law became one of the centers of the counterrevolution, perverting justice for reactionary political ends. "It is impossible to escape the conclusion," the historian Franz L. Neumann declared, "that political justice is the blackest page in the life of the German Republic." After the Kapp putsch in 1920 the government charged 705 persons with high treason; only one, the police president of Berlin, received a sentence—five years of "honorary confinement." When the state of Prussia withdrew his pension the Supreme Court ordered it restored. A German court in December 1926 awarded General Von Luettwitz, the military leader of the Kapp putsch, back payment of his pension to cover the period when he was a rebel against the government and also the five years that he was a fugitive from justice in Hungary.

## Inconsistent Justice

Yet hundreds of German liberals were sentenced to long prison terms on charges of treason because they revealed or denounced in the press or by speech the Army's constant violations of the Versailles Treaty. The treason laws were ruthlessly applied to the supporters of the Republic; those on the Right who tried to overthrow it, as Adolf Hitler was soon to learn, got off either free or with the lightest of sentences. Even the assassins, if they were of the Right and their victims democrats, were leniently treated by the courts or, as often happened, helped to escape from the custody of the courts by Army officers and right-wing extremists.

And so the mild Socialists, aided by the democrats and

the Catholic Centrists, were left to carry on the Republic, which tottered from its birth. They bore the hatred, the abuse and sometimes the bullets of their opponents, who grow in number and in resolve. "In the heart of the people," cried Oswald Spengler, who had skyrocketed to fame with his book *The Decline of the West,* "the Weimar Constitution is already doomed." Down in Bavaria the young firebrand Adolf Hitler grasped the strength of the new nationalist, antidemocratic, antirepublican tide. He began to ride it.

---

*The German delegation at Versailles wrote the unbending Clemenceau that such a treaty was "intolerable for any nation."*

---

He was greatly aided by the course of events, two in particular: the fall of the mark and the French occupation of the Ruhr. The mark, as we have seen, had began to slide in 1921, when it dropped to 75 to the dollar; the next year it fell to 400 and by the beginning of 1923 to 7,000. Already in the fall of 1922 the German government had asked the Allies to grant a moratorium on reparation payments. This the French government of Poincaré had bluntly refused. When Germany defaulted in deliveries of timber, the hard-headed French Premier, who had been the wartime President of France, ordered French troops to occupy the Ruhr. The industrial heart of Germany, which, after the loss of Upper Silesia to Poland, furnished the Reich with four fifths of its coal and steel production, was cut off from the rest of the country.

This paralyzing blow to Germany's economy united the people momentarily as they had not been united since 1914. The workers of the Ruhr declared a general strike and received financial support from the government in Berlin, which called for a campaign of passive resistance. With the help of the Army, sabotage and guerrilla warfare were organized. The French countered with arrests, deportations and even death sentences. But not a wheel in the Ruhr turned.

The strangulation of Germany's economy hastened the final plunge of the mark. On the occupation of the Ruhr in January 1923, it fell to 18,000 to the dollar; by July 1 it had dropped to 160,000; by August I to a million. By November, when Hitler thought his hour had struck, it took four billion marks to buy a dollar, and thereafter the figures became trillions. German currency had become utterly worthless. Purchasing power of salaries and wages was reduced to zero. The life savings of the middle classes and the working classes were wiped out. But something even more important was destroyed: the faith of the people in the economic structure of German society. What good were the standards and practices of such a society, which encouraged savings and investment and solemnly promised a safe return from them and then defaulted? Was this not a fraud upon the people?

And was not the democratic Republic, which had surrendered to the enemy and accepted the burden of reparations, to blame for the disaster? Unfortunately for its survival, the Republic did bear a responsibility. The inflation could have been halted by merely balancing the budget—a difficult but not impossible feat. Adequate taxation might have achieved this, but the new government did not dare to tax adequately. After all, the cost of the war—164 billion marks—had been met not even in part by direct taxation but 93 billions of it by war loans, 29 billions out of Treasury bills and the rest by increasing the issue of paper money. Instead of drastically raising taxes on those who could pay, the republican government actually reduced them in 1921.

---

*In the heart of the people the Weimar Constitution is already doomed.*

---

From then on, goaded by the big industrialists and landlords, who stood to gain though the masses of the people were financially ruined, the government deliberately let the mark tumble in order to free the State of its public debts, to escape from paying reparations and to sabotage the French in the Ruhr. Moreover, the destruction of the currency enabled German heavy industry to wipe out its indebtedness by refunding its obligations in worthless marks. The General Staff, disguised as the "Truppenamt" (Office of Troops) to evade the peace treaty which supposedly had outlawed it, took notice that the fall of the mark wiped out the war debts and thus left Germany financially unencumbered for a new war.

The masses of the people, however, did not realize how much the industrial tycoons, the Army and the State were benefiting from the ruin of the currency. All they knew was that a large bank account could not buy a straggly bunch of carrots, a half peck of potatoes, a few ounces of sugar, a pound of flour. They knew that as individuals they were bankrupt. And they knew hunger when it gnawed at them, as it did daily. In their misery and hopelessness they made the Republic the scapegoat for all that had happened.

Such times were heaven-sent for Adolf Hitler.

# 2

# Germans Believed Their Nation Had Been Betrayed

Peter Gay

At the end of World War I, a revolution overthrew German Kaiser Wilhelm II and, in the face of widespread street violence from both right-wing "Freikorps" and left-wing "Spartacists," German liberals formed the Weimar Republic. According to Peter Gay, the author of the following selection, the new Weimar government had worthy goals but failed to truly transform German society. Moreover, since Weimar representatives signed the Treaty of Versailles, they were considered to be the "November criminals" who had stabbed Germany in the back by accepting an unjust and humiliating peace.

Peter Gay is professor of history at Yale University.

---

H istorians have made much of the failures of the politicians who governed the young Republic. Had they failed utterly, it would have been understandable; [Weimar President Friedrich] Ebert and his associates faced difficulties that would have daunted the coolest and most experienced statesman. There was endemic disorder, there was desperate hunger, there was demoralization among intellectuals, there was an army to be brought home and demobilized, there were bitter wounds to be healed and no time to heal them, there was a constitution to be written and put into practice. And beyond this there was a factor which holds a special place in Weimar history, for the myths that

Excerpted from *Weimar Culture: The Outsider as Insider*, by Peter Gay (New York: Harper & Row). Copyright © 1968 by Peter Gay. Reprinted by permission of the author.

surrounded it came to hurt the Republic even more than reality: the Peace of Versailles.

---

*Some among the leading Allied negotiators*
*wanted not settlement but revenge.*

---

Certainly the settlement imposed on Germany at Versailles was in many ways a harsh and vindictive treaty. Some among the leading Allied negotiators wanted not settlement but revenge; it was not defeat alone that produced traumas—victory, too, after years of frustration, bloodshed, and endless misery, seemed to many somehow unbearable. The making of the treaty was a constant and deliberate humiliation of the Germans. Once the Allies had worked out their differences in a series of compromises, they invited the Germans in mid-April 1919 to send a delegation to Versailles to "receive peace conditions." Their task was to sign, not to negotiate. The treatment of the German delegation, widely publicized in the German press, was one long calculated insult: the train that took them to Paris moved with deliberate slowness through the battlefields of northern France until the sight became unbearable; once in Versailles, the Germans found themselves fenced off, ostensibly to be protected from hostile demonstrations, actually to be isolated from Allied negotiators. The Germans, writes M.J. Bonn, a liberal economist who was a member of the German delegation, "were greatly humiliated. The anguish of defeat and the sense of guilt with which some propagandists had tried to impress them had created a kind of inferiority complex from which most members of the delegation suffered." In his formal presentation of the treaty, [French Premier] Clemenceau did not make the Germans feel any better, and the short time they got to compile their comments and objections—first two weeks, and then a week more—threw the delegation into a frenzy of despairing activity. The outcome was quite inescapable: a combination of vehement protests, reasoned argument, and second thoughts on the part of [British prime minister] Lloyd George and [allied commander] General Smuts produced some marginal modifications, but in its essence the treaty remained unaltered. Germany was to lose Alsace-Lorraine, the Polish Corridor, northern

Schleswig-Holstein, and some other smaller areas—about 13 percent of its old territory, six millions in population, valuable resources—and all its colonies. It was to disarm, to pay reparations, and to sign a treaty that contained, as its article No. 231, the acknowledgment that Germany and its allies were "originators" of the war, and "aggressors"—that notorious paragraph that came to be called the "war guilt clause," and caused more debate, perhaps, than all other provisions together.

## Germany Had No Choice

What could the Germans do? They refused to sign, and they signed. On May 12, Prime Minister Scheidemann had called the treaty unacceptable and asked, rhetorically, "What hand must not wither which puts these fetters on itself and on us?" Scheidemann's hand remained intact; on June 20, after the Catholic Center Party and a majority of his own Social Democratic Party voted to accept the treaty with the exception of article 231 and the article demanding the handing over of war criminals, he resigned. The burden of signing the *Diktat*, the *Schandfrieden*, the *Schmachfrieden*—the shameful, humiliating peace—fell on the shoulders of other Social Democrats, and on Erzberger, the most prominent advocate of peace in the Center Party. They were brave men, accepting as their lot a political liability they would never wholly shake off.

Everyone hated the treaty; those who advocated its acceptance put their argument on grounds of realism—the need for peace, the starvation among the German population, the intransigence of the Allies. The *Frankfurter Zeitung*, the voice of reason at all times, was typical of the best opinion: it protested against the treaty but then urged that it be signed. [Novelist] Thomas Mann, not yet committed to the Republic, thought that Clemenceau, that "poisonous old man," was burying Western culture, or, conversely, that the dominance of Anglo-America would bring "the civilizing, rationalizing, utilitarianizing of the West"— in either event, the peace was a catastrophe. He was still the unpolitical, cultural aristocrat he had been before and during the war, but Count Kessler, liberal statesman and indefatigable diarist, eminently well informed and remarkably free from caste prejudice, also found Versailles infinitely depressing: from May 7, 1919, the day the Germans were

handed the conditions of peace, to June 12, he was so dis-
heartened that he wrote nothing in his diary; on June 22, after the resignation of the Scheidemann cabinet, he reported
a general mood of "indescribable dejection; as though all
life in the soul had died." The comments of patriots, army
officers, conservatives, can be imagined. All states and all
nations, Friedrich Meinecke wrote in 1921, must say to
themselves, "We are sinners." But "the sins committed by
the Allies since 1918 are almost without parallel."

It was this attitude much more than the provisions of
the treaty—bad as they were—that saddled the Weimar Republic with one of its many damaging legends. Millions who
had no stake in the lost colonies or the lost territories, who
were untouched by the enforced disarmament, responded
warmly to the demagogues who denounced Versailles as a
typical French attack on the very soul of Germany and ma-
ligned the signers of the treaty as cowards or traitors, and
had little but contempt for the statesmen who worked quietly to revise the treaty article by article. The demand for
abrogation of the "dictated peace," and punishment of the
"November criminals" who had accepted it, became the sta-
ple of right-wing rhetoric, and, with anti-Semitism, the
most prominent point in Nazi propaganda. If Versailles was
a burden on Weimar, the burden was as much of domestic
as of foreign manufacture.

---

*The peace was a catastrophe.*

---

In the light of all this, the revolution and its aftermath
accomplished a great deal. It ended the war. It swept away—
forever—the Prussian ruling house and the other German
monarchies, large and small. It educated at least some Germans in the ways of practical politics. It established a democratic state. It gave new opportunities to talent ineligible
for preferment in the Empire, opening centers of prestige
and power to progressive professors, modern playwrights
and producers, democratic political thinkers. Hugo Preuss,
the architect of the Weimar Constitution, was a symbol of
the revolution; as a Jew and a left-wing democrat, he had
been kept out of the university establishment for all his merits, and now he, the outsider, gave shape to the new Republic, *his* Republic.

## The Failures of Postwar German Leaders

Yet, when all allowances have been made, it remains true that the men of Weimar made grievous mistakes, and recriminations over them poisoned the atmosphere early, preparing the way for further mistakes. The brilliant political journalist Carl von Ossietzky summed it up as early as June 1919: "There were three areas in which we had a right to expect an absolute break with old methods, and reconstruction: in the purely political, the economic, and the spiritual-ethical area." But "what has the revolution accomplished? The answer is sad indeed. In foreign and domestic politics celebrities swagger around who for several decades have of right belonged in a reliquary. Economic reconstruction is steadily being postponed, while anarchy, egotism, profiteering triumph. No resisting hand, only soft persuasion. Poverty of ideas, lack of courage, lack of faith." It is a stern indictment, but not without justice. The republicans' search for order, their fear of Bolshevism, the timidity of leaders themselves the product of the old society and better equipped to oppose than to govern—and, it must be added, the confusion, irresponsibility, bloodthirsty language, and dictatorial pretensions of the Spartacist left—forestalled decisive action in area after area. Preuss, gravely worried by the hegemony of Prussia, wanted to destroy the old federal collection of states, break up Prussia into several *Länder* [states], and gather a number of small states into larger units. His plan was not adopted, and among its most effective adversaries were Social Democrats, unwilling to yield what they had just acquired, or—as with Eisner in Bavaria—suspicious of the central regime. A compromise kept the old states intact, preserved Prussian dominance, and left the troublesome relations between the Reich and the *Länder* unappeased. "It remains a historical sin of omission," the Socialist editor and politician Friedrich Stampfer conceded later, his hindsight working at full capacity, "that in that time of stormy, progressive development the leap into the unitary state was not taken. Despite all Platonic obeisances to the idea of national unity, some social-democratic holders of power defended particular interests with an eagerness no less intense than that shown earlier by the dynasts." The affair was to provide a painful lesson to Socialists jealous of their office: a short-range parochial gain proved to be a long-range public disaster.

The nationalization of major industries had the same

history; ambitious schemes and goodwill were never translated into policy. The economist Rudolph Wissell pointed out the road to socialism through planning, and the road was clear enough. But it was never taken. Big industry proceeded to "nationalize" the economy in its own way—through cartelization. Indeed, "the largest trusts in German history were formed during the Weimar Republic," including the merger in 1926 of four large steel companies, and the formation of the chemical trust, I.G. Farben, the year before, through a merger of "the six largest corporations in this field." The Socialists stood by, either too timid to act or in the doctrinaire and unrealistic conviction that cartelization was an inevitable higher stage of capitalism which must be traversed on the road to socialism. In relying on history, German Socialists became its victim.

These were fateful strategic mistakes, but the men of Weimar made an even more fateful mistake when they failed to tame, or transform, the machinery of the old order—the military, the civil service, and the courts. The military caste had come out of the war demoralized, its prestige shattered, in panic, ready for any compromise. The generals had led Germany into disaster, lying to themselves as much as to the world, wasting uncounted lives. Friedrich Meinecke acknowledged late in 1918 that "the unmeasured claims of the pan-German-militarist-conservative combine" had utterly discredited them." Yet within a few years this combine had regained its charisma for wide circles of the public and burdened the Republic with the legend of an undefeated German Army stabbed in the back at home by Jews and Communists—the notorious *Dolchstosslegende*.

# 3

# German Reactions to the Treaty Were Understandable

Samuel W. Mitcham Jr.

In the following selection historian Samuel W. Mitcham Jr. traces the process by which the Treaty of Versailles was presented to German representatives and how, with great reluctance and following a period of political upheaval, the parliament of the Weimar Republic finally approved it in the face of an Allied ultimatum threatening renewed warfare. Mitcham notes that Germans had cause to object to the treaty almost from its beginning. German officials were neither permitted to negotiate any of the terms nor to include formal objections to any of its provisions. The author concludes by suggesting that had the Allies been less vindictive, the Weimar Republic might have had a stronger chance of survival.

Samuel W. Mitcham Jr. is the author of more than a dozen books on Nazi Germany and World War II.

---

In April 1919 the German government issued its directives to its delegates attending the peace conference, which had at last been scheduled to convene in Paris the following month. The instructions emphasized the fact that the German government regarded Wilson's Fourteen Points as binding on both sides, and they would have to be the basis of any settlement. Among other things, the Germans wanted a free plebiscite in Alsace-Lorraine, Posen, and northern Schleswig; the evacuation of German territory un-

Excerpted from *Why Hitler? The Genesis of the Nazi Reich*, by Samuel W. Mitcham Jr. Copyright © 1996 by Samuel W. Mitcham Jr. Reproduced with permission from Greenwood Publishing Group, Westport, CT.

der Allied occupation when the treaty was concluded; the formation of a League of Nations to settle international disputes by arbitration; a prompt lifting of the blockade; and the return of the German merchant marine and of all German colonies lost during the war. They agreed to pay reparations for civilian losses and civilian property damage. They unequivocally denied that Germany alone was responsible for the war and rejected the cession of Upper Silesia or of a Polish Corridor through Prussia to the sea.

The chief of the German delegation was Count Ulrich von Brockdorff-Rantzau, a man of genuine liberal views who had served for years as an Imperial ambassador, most recently at Copenhagen. Not affiliated with any political party, he had accepted the post of foreign minister in December 1918 with the stipulation that the Allies' peace conditions could be rejected if they would not allow the German people the chance to lead half-way decent lives.

The German representatives arrived in Paris on April 29, 1919, and their reception was anything but friendly. They were kept practically under house arrest until May 7, when the Allies were at last ready to meet with them. The terms of the peace treaty were handed to the German delegation at Trianon, not far from the Palace of Versailles, where Bismarck had proclaimed the creation of the second German Empire (*Reich*) on January 18, 1871. Georges Clemenceau, the French premier, rose and briefly addressed the Germans, while copies of the 70,000-word document (which he called the "Second Treaty of Versailles") were passed out. Then Foreign Minister von Brockdorff was given a few minutes to respond. He remained seated because he had severe stage fright (he said later) and did not trust his knees; the Allies, however, took it as a gesture of arrogance and were livid. Brockdorff-Rantzau spoke bitterly about "the hundreds of thousands of noncombatants starved by the blockade since November 11" and deplored how they had deliberately been killed after the Allies had won their victory. This speech was not what the Allied leaders wanted to hear. Clemenceau's face turned red with rage and Lloyd George, the British prime minister, broke a letter opener on the desk in front of him. After Brockdorff concluded his remarks, he was tersely informed that the Germans had 15 days to read the treaty and to prepare any objections, questions, or counterproposals they had in writing, but only in

French or English. Oral discussions and verbal communications were forbidden, as was any response in German.

These high-handed tactics were a serious blunder. Excluding the Germans from the peace process until the treaty was drafted and then refusing to verbally discuss it with them lent considerable credibility to the charge that it was a dictated peace. Even Woodrow Wilson, who had been voted down by his former allies, said that, if he were a German, he would not sign it. When he saw the treaty, Marshal Foch, who certainly had no love for the Germans, exclaimed: "This is not a peace treaty. It is a 20 years' truce." It was also a punitive peace, for the terms of the treaty were harsh, to say the least. Alsace and Lorraine were to be ceded to France without a plebiscite. The German territory west of the Rhine presently under Allied occupation—including the cities of Cologne, Koblenz, and Mainz—was to be occupied by Allied troops for at least 15 years, although they might evacuate it piecemeal if Germany fulfilled all of her treaty obligations. The right bank of the Rhine was to be permanently demilitarized for a distance of 50 kilometers. The Saar basin—a clearly German area that possessed some of the richest coal deposits in Europe—was to be administered by a League of Nations commission for 15 years, during which the French would be in charge of the mines; thereafter it might be returned to Germany by a plebiscite. If the Saar voted to return to the Reich, Germany would have to purchase the mines. The districts of Moresnet, Eupen, and Malmedy were to be turned over to Belgium; Schleswig would choose by plebiscite whether it wanted to be German or Danish. (Ultimately it was split, with northern Schleswig voting to join Denmark.)

## Unfair Military and Economic Restrictions

In the east, Germany was to hand over the rich (and largely German) industrial area of Upper Silesia to France's ally, Poland, along with most of Posen and West Prussia. The so-called Polish Corridor would cut across Germany to the Baltic, giving Poland access to the sea and completely severing East Prussia from the rest of the Reich. The city of Danzig was to be set up as a Free City under the administration of the League of Nations, despite the fact that its population was 95 percent German—a clear violation of the Wilsonian principle of self-determination. The Poles would have extensive economic and trade rights in the Free City. In addition, Germany would have to give up the East Prussian city of Memel (which eventually became part of Lithuania). In all, Germany would lose one-eighth of its national territory. None of her colonies would be returned. The treaty also forbade an *Anschluss* (union) between Germany and Austria, as did the Treaty of Saint Germain (the peace treaty between the Allies and Austria).

---

*Excluding the Germans from the peace process until the treaty was drafted and then refusing to verbally discuss it with them lent considerable credibility to the charge that it was a dictated peace.*

---

In addition, the Treaty of Versailles sought to reduce Germany to a state of military impotence. Germany would have to reduce its army—still 500,000 strong, excluding the Freikorps—to 100,000 men, of which only 4,000 could be officers. Officers would have to sign up for terms of 25 years and the enlistment for other ranks would be 12 years—provisions designed to prevent Germany from establishing a significant military reserve. The types of weapons the army could have were severely curtailed, and all excess war materials were to be surrendered to the Allies. The treaty went so far as to specify how many rounds of ammunition the army could have in reserve, and even German hunting clubs were to be regulated, to eliminate them as a potential source of paramilitary training. The great General Staff would be dissolved, and the elite cadet school at Gross-Lichterfeld was to be closed, along with most other training establishments. Of the four great weapons innovations of World War I (tanks, poisonous gas, the airplane, and the submarine), Germany was to be denied all four. The German Navy was to be reduced to what Halperin called "innocuous proportions": 6 small battleships, 6 light cruisers, 12 destroyers, 12 torpedo boats, and a few coastal guns. An Inter-Allied Control Commission was to be set up to ensure German compliance with the military clauses of the treaty. It would have the right to go anywhere on German soil to conduct inspections on demand, at German expense.

The commercial articles of the treaty were as unfair as the others. In these clauses, the Allies granted themselves most-favored-nation status in the German market, but without reciprocation. All commercial agreements that allowed Germany to trade with other countries on advantageous terms were abrogated, thus effectively barring German products from Allied markets. These clauses would deny Germany—already saddled with a huge war debt—the ability to accumulate foreign capital and cut her off from one of her few potential sources of revenue. As if this were not enough, almost all of her foreign financial holdings were to be confiscated and her merchant fleet reduced to less than one-tenth its prewar size. In addition, German shipyards would have to construct 200,000 tons of new shipping per year and hand it over to the Allies, free of charge.

Germany also had to agree to pay whatever reparations the Allies demanded, even though the exact amount to be paid had yet to be determined. Germany, in effect, would have to sign a blank check worth billions.

Finally came the so-called "shame paragraphs." Germany would have to assume sole responsibility for starting the war—something she clearly did not do; in fact, Germany was the last of the major European powers to mobilize in 1914. Also, Germany would have to agree to hand over to the Allies anyone they decided to try as a "war criminal" and would have to assist the Allies in compiling evidence against these people. Finally, Germany would not be granted admission into the League of Nations.

Up until this point, most Germans had deluded themselves into believing that they would receive a just peace; the Allies had, after all, led them to believe the treaty would be based on Wilson's Fourteen Points. Now their final illusions were shattered. "The unbelievable has happened," Reichstag President Konstantin Fehrenbach exclaimed. "Our enemies have presented us with a treaty which surpasses the worst fears of our greatest pessimists." President Ebert denounced the treaty as "unbearable," and Chancellor Scheidemann instructed Brockdorff to inform the Allies that the terms were unfulfillable and would ruin Germany. Simultaneously, he issued a proclamation denouncing the treaty and forcefully pointed out that it was not in accordance with the promises made prior to the armistice. "May the hand wither that signs such a treaty!" he cried. For the first time in years,

Germans of every class and every political persuasion were united on one issue: They had been deceived by men who had never had the slightest intention of honoring their pledges. Throughout the war, the Allied leaders had declared that they were waging war against the House of Hohenzollern, not against the German people; now the German civilians unanimously felt that they had been lied to. Countless mass meetings were held, and protests were widespread. All forms of public entertainment were suspended for a week, and a period of official mourning ensued.

---

*Throughout the war, the Allied leaders had declared that they were waging war against the House of Hohenzollern, not against the German people; now the German civilians unanimously felt that they had been lied to.*

---

The German public reaction to the treaty caused the Allies to hesitate and even to offer a few concessions. The deadline for German acceptance was extended to June 23; though the Saar was under Allied occupation, its local governments could now be administered by Germans, but the French still got the mines; and the area subject to plebiscite in Schleswig was reduced somewhat. Most significantly, the Allies agreed that the fate of Upper Silesia would be determined by a plebiscite, rather than by outright concession to the Poles. Nevertheless, the protests continued throughout Germany. However, protesting an unjust treaty was one thing; refusing to sign it was something else altogether, for the alternative to signing was going back to war, and this Germany could not do. Most of the German Army had already gone home, but the Allies—especially the French— had the means to resume the conflict very quickly and were clearly prepared to do so. Also, in accordance with the terms of the armistice, the army had evacuated its foreign-held territory and had given the Allies major bridgeheads across the Rhine. If the war resumed, it would be fought on German territory. Nevertheless, at Versailles, Foreign Minister von Brockdorff berated the treaty and urged its rejection. He then informed the Allies that he was returning to Weimar. As he left, he and the German delegation were stoned by an angry French mob.

When Count von Brockdorff arrived at the German capital on the morning of June 18, he found the cabinet and every political party sharply divided. Some, like Chancellor Scheidemann, adamantly opposed signing. Others, while expressing dismay at the treaty, were even more dismayed about the prospect of resuming the war. This could mean the rise of separatism, especially in Bavaria (Germany had only united 48 years previously, after all); renewed Bolshevik uprisings; and the eventual disintegration of the Republic which would, in the end, be forced to sign anyway. Gustav Noske, who was very worried about more Red uprisings, was in favor of signing, but it was Matthias Erzberger who took the lead in urging ratification. After considerable debate, Noske signaled the High Command (now headquartered in Kolberg) and asked what the prospects of armed resistance were. Hindenburg replied that the army could resist successfully in the east, but not in the west, where French and American armies were poised to invade. He called upon the administration to reject the treaty anyway; as a soldier, he said, he preferred honorable annihilation to a dishonorable peace. After receiving this message, the Social Democrats joined the Centrists in supporting ratification.

## Germans Reluctantly Approve the Treaty

The result was yet another governmental crisis. Chancellor Scheidemann, could not support his party's position and resigned, leaving Germany without a government—three days before the Allied deadline (and with it the armistice) expired. Ebert had a difficult time finding someone to form a new government. He turned to Otto Landsberg, but he refused to have anything to do with the treaty, even though his stand meant giving up the chancellorship. Finally, with the expiration of the deadline only 24 hours away, Ebert was rescued by a Centrist-Social Democratic coalition under Gustav Bauer, the former minister of labor. Ulrich von Brockdorff-Rantzau resigned in protest and was replaced as foreign minister by Hermann Müller. Field Marshal von Hindenburg and his deputy, General Groener, the chief of the General Staff and the Quartermaster-General of the army, respectively, announced their retirements. Matthias Erzberger, the man who had originally signed the armistice and who led the proponents of the treaty, was named minister of finance in the new cabinet.

On June 22, 1919, the German Reichstag ratified the Treaty of Versailles by a vote of 237 to 138. Many Social Democrats, most notably Scheidemann and Landsberg, were absent. The German resolution contained two exceptions: the shame paragraphs (which stated that German aggression was solely responsible for the war) and the war criminals paragraphs. The Allies refused to accept even this. Finally, only 19 minutes before the Allied ultimatum ran out, the German delegation capitulated and informed the French that the Reich accepted the treaty under duress. It was signed in the Hall of Mirrors in the Palace of Versailles on the afternoon of June 28, 1919—the very room in which the German Empire had been declared in 1871. Hermann Müller and Dr. Hans Bell, the Centrist minister of transportation, signed for the Weimar Republic.

The Treaty of Versailles dealt the Weimar Republic a blow from which it never fully recovered. "Instead of using their powers as victors to help democracy in Germany," historian [Samuel Halperin] wrote,

> the Allies made its position infinitely more difficult. They refused to recognize the fact that the November revolution had transformed the Reich into a state in which the people were sovereign. They treated as of no account the impressive victory which moderate republicanism had won in the elections of January, 1919. They persisted in regarding the Germany of Ebert and Scheidemann as in no essential regard different from the Junker-dominated Germany of 1914. What they failed to see was that the consolidation of democracy in Germany was the first prerequisite of European and world peace. In their anxiety to weaken and fetter Germany, they overlooked the all-important fact that nowhere were there stauncher believers in Wilsonian idealism than the men and women who composed the parties of the Weimar coalition.

Professor Abel of Columbia University would have agreed with the above statement. He wrote:

> In retrospect it is clear that the affair of the Versailles Treaty was the primary factor in the debacle of democracy in Germany. It discredited the leaders who for

months maintained that only a new, democratic Germany could count upon a just peace from the Western democracies. This became the mainspring of all subsequent attacks on the republican regime.

Another historian [William Shirer] went even further and called World War II "the war over the settlement of Versailles," and Eliot Barculo Wheaton wrote:

> quite aside from the question of practicability, the crushing nature of the Versailles terms was unwise, for it gave German extremists the most combustible material wherewith to inflame nationalist passions and perpetuate a sense of cruel injury.

At least two Allied leaders at the time would have agreed with Wheaton. Winston Churchill denounced the economic clauses as "malignant and silly," and Woodrow Wilson said of the treaty: "If I were a German, I think I should not sign it."

Niccolo Machiavelli advised the prince to never inflict small hurts. This is exactly what the Allies did with the armistice and the Treaty of Versailles. The German people were humiliated, and their faith in democracy—which was fragile to begin with—was almost totally destroyed. However, they were not annihilated. Their industrial plants remained largely intact, their skilled workers and inventors remained valuable assets, their young men remained warlike and military-oriented, their talent in technological and military matters remained unimpaired, and their extreme nationalism—which they were in the process of abandoning in late 1918—had been thoroughly and fatefully restored. The Allies should have either totally destroyed and dismembered Germany or else have made a sincere effort to make a fair and just peace with her and bring her into the family of nations as a full partner. By doing neither, they set the stage for Adolf Hitler and the Second World War. In my view, it is not going too far to state that the Nazi dictator should have worn a stamp on the seat of his pants with three words on it: "Made at Versailles."

# 4

# The Failures of the Peacemakers

Charles L. Mee Jr.

In the following selection, Charles L. Mee Jr. examines the costs of the First World War and the Treaty of Versailles to Europe in general but also to the politicians who attempted to conclude a reasonable peace. The author suggests that the Treaty of Versailles, which Woodrow Wilson, Lloyd George, Clemenceau, and the founders of the German Weimar Republic spent much of their careers trying—but failing—to justify, was the last gasp of Europe's nineteenth-century order. The treaty's failures indicated that the world's problems could no longer be solved by a narrow elite of politicians and aristocrats.

Charles L. Mee Jr. is a historian and journalist whose books include *Meeting at Potsdam* and *Seizure*.

W hen all the diplomats had dispersed at last, and the Palace of Versailles was left to the gardeners, and the delegations returned once more to their homelands, the Europe that they left behind still trembled with the wounds and shocks of war and the insults of peace.

A generation had been decimated on the battlefields of Europe. No one had seen the likes of such slaughter before: the deaths of soldiers per day of battle were 10 times greater than in the American Civil War, 24 times the deaths in the Napoleonic Wars, 550 times the deaths in the Boer War. And still the epidemic of flu spread through Europe and America and elsewhere until it had claimed another 14 million lives among the survivors of the war.

The economy of Europe was in ruins. Food prices had risen during the war by 103 percent in Rome, by 106 percent in Paris, by 110 percent in London, and, in Germany, prices had become all but meaningless. The Germans had 40 percent less butter than in 1914, 42 percent less meat, 50 percent less milk. The destruction of factories, railroads, and shipping produced economic dislocation on such an order as to be excruciating.

## Economic and Political Dangers

Even before the treaty had been signed, the so-called Vilna dispute had erupted into a pocket war. The Polish general Joseph Pilsudski took the town of Vilna from the Bolsheviks; diplomatic negotiations returned the town to the Bolsheviks—who only had it taken from them by the Lithuanians who were driven out by a band of Polish freebooters.

The Teschen conflict, too, commenced before the Paris conference had adjourned, and then the Polish-Russian War broke out, and then the Burgenland dispute between Austria and Hungary over a strip of territory predominantly inhabited by Germans but occupied by Hungarian irregulars and assigned by the pence conference to Austria.

On June 22, 1920, Greece, encouraged by Lloyd George, invaded Anatolia, and Turkey invaded Armenia. In Italy, Gabriele d'Annunzio led an expedition into Fiume. The Italians negotiated with the Yugoslavs and gave up Fiume—but a Fascist coup overthrew the government and forced Yugoslavia to abandon its claims.

Anxiety led to the formation of the kind of interlocking set of alliances in which the world had been caught in 1914. In February of 1920, France and Poland signed a pact to come to one another's assistance in case of attack; in March of 1920, Poland and Rumania signed a defense treaty. Several weeks later, Germany was said to be in default on some of its war debts; the French occupied Düsseldorf, Duisburg, and Ruhrort. In April, Rumania joined Czechoslovakia in the Little Entente.

The war had cost $603.57 billion. Rubber was in such short supply in Europe that trucks were traveling on their rims, and fats were so scarce that housewives strained their dishwater to salvage whatever grease it might contain. International trade was in shambles: British exports were only half what they had been before the war. By 1921, the world

economy had stumbled into a brief, but portentous, depression, distinguished not by uniformity but by apparent
caprice. While the manufacture of gas masks and airplane
wings ceased, the production of copper and wheat continued at such vigorous wartime levels that prices slumped
precipitately.

And then inflation struck. In Germany, to pay for the
war, the money in circulation had been quintupled; public
debt was 20 times its prewar level. The exchange was 4 marks
to the dollar in 1914, then 14.8 marks to the dollar in May of
1921, then 62.6 marks to the dollar in November of 1921,
and then 62 *billion* marks to the dollar in October of 1923.

Prices soared. Money was worthless, as were insurance
policies and savings accounts. The mortgage on a house was
worth less, in paper marks, than a glass of beer.

As for war debts, in 1921, the reparations commission
finally fixed Germany's debt at 132 billion gold marks to be
paid over 30 years, plus 26 percent of the proceeds of German exports and some other goods—an assessment that, by
1922, was manifestly absurd. The Germans defaulted. On
January 11, 1923, French and Belgian troops moved in to
occupy the Ruhr district.

---

*Prices soared. Money was worthless, as were
insurance policies and savings accounts. The
mortgage on a house was worth less, in paper
marks, than a glass of beer.*

---

The Germans, in retaliation for the French military
move, purposely set about inflating their currency; and the
effects of German inflation spread. The French franc fell by
25 percent. An American banker, Charles Dawes, was called
in to stave off disaster, and the Dawes Plan, postponing and
reducing German payments, prolonged the agony.

Within the changing context of all these rising and
falling currencies, Germany eventually paid 36 billion gold
marks. In the same period, Germany borrowed from foreign sources about 33 billion marks that were, for the most
part, never repaid. The actual effect of reparations, then,
was economically negligible. Nonetheless, because the Germans believed that reparations debts, whether paid or not,

were the cause of their economic troubles, the effect of the reparations clauses of the Versailles treaty was fiercely embittering to the Germans.

By 1925, France had signed treaties with both Poland and Czechoslovakia for mutual assistance in case of attack by Germany. The Weimar government in Germany had settled down to a tenuous existence, while the Protestant middle classes drifted toward the reactionary right. And gradually the world slid into the great depression of the thirties, the Japanese invasion of Manchuria, the Italian attack on Ethiopia, the German reoccupation of the Rhineland.

## A Broken U.S. President

At the conclusion of the Paris conference, Wilson returned from Europe to do battle with the United States Senate over ratification of the treaty. Colonel House had advised the president, just before Wilson sailed for America, to be conciliatory to his Senate opponents. Of ninety-six senators, only fourteen Republicans and four Democrats were unalterably opposed to the treaty—and the majority of American citizens favored its adoption. But, before Wilson boarded the *George Washington* he said to the colonel: "House, I have found one can never get anything in this life that is worthwhile without fighting for it."

In Washington, Wilson scorned the meddlesome efforts of the Senate to "advise and consent." Some senators suggested some minor revisions—a clause, for example, that would explicitly note that the United States, as a member of the League of Nations, would not come to the aid of another country in war without an express declaration of war from Congress. Wilson would have none of it. Rather than woo the "mild reservationists" to his side by accepting their suggestions, he drove them over to the side of the "irreconcilables" by insisting that the treaty be taken just as it was, without changing a comma.

In September, the president set out on a twenty-seven-day crusade across America to persuade the American people to force the Senate to "take its medicine." He traveled eight thousand miles, he delivered forty speeches, and attended lunches, receptions, dinners. When he had left Washington, he was suffering from ferocious headaches, and his hands were shaking. As he went from town to town, the headaches became increasingly persistent, until he was in constant pain. Urged by Mrs. Wilson and Dr. Grayson [his physician] and others to stop and rest, Wilson drove himself on, until, in Pueblo, Colorado, he was stopped by a stroke that paralyzed an arm and a leg. And then, soon after, he was assaulted by another stroke that paralyzed his entire body and deprived him of his speech.

He was returned to the White House where he recovered and languished, rose to lucidity and disintegrated in fits of bitterness, while Mrs. Wilson attended to the duties of the presidency in his name. The treaty was defeated in the Senate—but its defeat provoked such a public clamor that the senators were persuaded to bring it up again, this time in a form sufficiently amended to assure its passage. For this second vote, Wilson roused himself to send a message to his Democratic supporters in the Senate—to vote *against* the revised treaty. As the roll call was taken, Senator Brandegee, one of the "irreconcilables," turned to Senator Lodge. "We can always depend on Mr. Wilson," said Brandegee. "He has never failed us." The treaty was defeated, by a narrow margin of only seven votes.

As the Republicans and Democrats geared up for the elections of 1920, Wilson evidently thought—in spite of his devastated mind, or because of it—that he would be called to run for an unprecedented third term as president. He waited for the call to come from the Democratic convention in San Francisco, but his name was not even put before the delegates. The Democrats nominated Governor James Cox of Ohio, who lost to Warren Harding, and Wilson moved out of the White House to another home in Washington. There he lingered, with Mrs. Wilson to care for him. In his last years, he grew increasingly dour and nasty. Sometimes he would receive friends in his study, and speak well for a time; occasionally he would deliver himself of a well-turned jest or pun or comment on politics; but often he would lapse into paroxysms of tears, spitefulness, or hatred.

He was certain, when he stirred himself to focus on such matters, that his opponents would finally bring themselves to "utter destruction" and to "contempt." He had, he said, "seen fools resist Providence before."

In the end, he sank into deep self-pitying depression. In January of 1924, when Dr. Grayson wanted to go off for a week's holiday, Wilson was profoundly depressed. Mrs. Wilson found him sitting in his room with his head bowed, and asked him if he felt badly. "I always feel badly now, little girl," he said wearily. She asked if he wanted Grayson to stay. No, he said, Grayson needed the holiday. But then, he said slowly, "it won't be very much longer, and I had hoped he would not desert me."

By early February, he could no longer move from his bed. Grayson, back from his vacation, came to see his old patient. "I am," Wilson said to the doctor, "a broken piece of machinery. When the machinery is broken—"

He died on February 3, 1924, at the age of sixty-seven.

## The Failures of Clemenceau and Lloyd George

Georges Clemenceau hoped to be rewarded for his efforts on behalf of France at the peace conference by being elected to the largely honorary office of president of the French republic. Instead, he was promptly attacked by President Poincaré, Marshal Foch, the army, and the right wing, for having sold out France at the conference by agreeing to a "soft" peace. At the same time, the socialists attacked him from the left for the way he had so rudely suppressed strikes and censored newspapers and curbed free speech during the war. Caught at last between the two warring factions of the French republic, finding that there were few old friends to comfort the erstwhile "wrecker of ministries," not only was Clemenceau kept from the office of president, but his own ministry was resoundingly renounced in the elections held in the autumn of 1919.

Clemenceau had resolved that he would never answer any criticism brought against his policies during the war or the peace conference, but in the end, he could not restrain himself. The problem, he wrote in *Grandeurs et Misères d'une Victoire*, was not with the treaty, but with the will of the government that succeeded his to see that the treaty was enforced. The treaty itself, for all its flaws, was good.

And yet, Clemenceau was not entirely satisfied with his defense of his actions. He revised his manuscript over and over, and could still not bring himself to rest content with his defense. Then, in mid-November of 1929, still fretting over his manuscript, he fell ill and took to his bed. His strength left him at once; he lapsed into a coma, and within a week he was dead, at the age of eighty-eight, his vindication still not finished to his satisfaction.

Lloyd George, soon after he returned from the conference to London, had to deal with nasty coal-mining and railroad strikes, and it became increasingly difficult to hide the fact that the war had had a devastating economic impact on Britain, and that reparations would not save the empire. Lloyd George tried budget cuts, an antiwaste campaign, and other improvisatory policies, but the electorate became increasingly impatient with him. In 1922, he tried to rescue his political fortunes by grandstanding, calling for an international conference in Genoa. This conference only resulted in a pact in which Russia ingratiated herself with the Germans by repudiating any claim for reparations.

Soon thereafter, it was discovered that one of Lloyd George's campaign fund-raising operations had engaged in some irregular practices. By October of 1922, he had lost his support in the House of Commons. A general election was called, and the prime minister's Liberal party was defeated, and never recovered.

He would not retire—and his faithful Carnarvonshire constituents returned him to office every time an election was called. Yet, Lloyd George's faction lost power with each election. In 1923, the Liberals held 159 of the 608 seats in the House of Commons. By 1929, Lloyd George's supporters numbered 59. His daughter Megan, his son Gwilym, and his son's brother-in-law Goronwy Owen all stood for election and won seats in Commons—but by 1931 they were Lloyd George's only followers. No one else trusted him any longer. He lived another fourteen years as a political castoff, still vexing both the right and the left by his mercurial ways.

---

*When [Brockdorff-Rantzau] died in 1928, his last words, spoken to his brother, were: "Do not mourn. After all, I have really been dead ever since Versailles."*

---

On the one hand, Lloyd George had misgivings about the treaty, and could not quite bring himself to criticize German rearmament in the thirties; on the other hand, he opposed "appeasement" of Germany. On the one hand, he was impressed by Hitler, visited the führer at Berchtesgaden and called him "the greatest living German"; but, on the other hand, he advocated closer cooperation with Russia in anticipation of danger from Germany. When war broke out in 1939, Lloyd George turned down Churchill's nostalgic offer of a cabinet position, criticized the group who had taken over the direction of Britain's destiny, thought Britain would lose the war, thought Churchill's government would fall, and turned down the offer of an ambassadorship. Still, he always accepted an invitation for luncheon or a conversation about his political future, evidently harboring the extraordinary hope that he would himself once again be called to lead the nation in war.

## Attacks on Weimar Leaders

Of the Germans, Friedrich Ebert was subjected to constant abuse from the right wing, and, in 1922, when he was called a traitor to his face, he sued for slander. The court found in his favor, although it declared that when he had called a strike against the Hohenzollern monarchy in 1918, he had been, in a certain narrow sense, a traitor. In time, Ebert was drawn into more lawsuits—he had slander suits out against 150 defendants at one point—and the ceaseless plague of accusations of treason and his retaliatory litigation undid his health, and his mind, and he died in 1925, after neglecting his doctor's diagnosis of appendicitis, of peritonitis.

Philipp Scheidemann remained a member of the Reichstag, where he made speeches warning against the rise of militarism in Germany. For his pains he was put on the list of the men who had consented to the armistice in 1918, the so-called November criminals, and two men attempted to murder him in June of 1922. Scheidemann, who always carried a pistol, fell to the ground firing and scared off the would-be assassins. Thereafter, he always traveled armed and in the company of armed friends. He died of natural causes in 1939.

Matthias Erzberger was charged with fiscal irresponsibility as minister of finance. He sued for libel, and, in the trial, he was subjected to much abuse for signing the armistice and encouraging acceptance of the treaty. After he resigned, he was not left alone until, in August of 1921, he was assassinated as a "November criminal."

Count von Brockdorff-Rantzau retired from the government for several years, until 1922, when he was persuaded to become ambassador to the Soviet Union, where he remained for six years. When he died, in 1928, his last words, spoken to his brother, were: "Do not mourn. After all, I have really been dead ever since Versailles."

As for the treaty itself, it was rejected by the Congress of the United States. It was formally accepted by the French, but only grudgingly, and was pilloried, beginning at once and continuously, by both the left and the right. Formally accepted by the English, the treaty was savaged at once by Keynes in his book *The Economic Consequences of the Peace*, which set off a sustained attack on the treaty by English liberals. English shame over the treaty provisions encouraged the Germans, increasingly, to believe that they could ignore or violate it with impunity. The treaty was despised in Germany, hated by the Japanese, not signed by the Chinese, and it was the subject of denunciatory expositions in school classrooms in Hungary, Austria, Yugoslavia, and the rest of Eastern Europe.

Through all this, Hitler rose to power. He made his first public impression, and he continued to draw audiences, and hold and augment them, by delivering the same speech over and over again: a vitriolic speech entitled "The Treaty of Versailles."

No single conclusion can be drawn from all this disaster without diminishing the experience of history itself. The lesson of Versailles is protean, not simple, and as the event is turned over in the mind, a hundred different nuances and shadings appear. The experience cannot be impaled on one moral or another. Yet, certain lessons suggest themselves with an undeniable insistence.

The first, surely, is a reminder of the double maxim: it is always easier to start a war than to end one, let alone win it. And the second is that harshness and vengeance nearly always return to haunt those who impose them.

But of all the lessons that Versailles leaves us, certainly the most insistent is that of the inability of the few any longer to govern the many. The few world rulers who dominated Versailles simply could not any longer settle the fate of the many new nations. The few old imperial powers could no longer impose their will on the many new peoples who took their destinies into their own hands. The few heads of state gathered in a small room could no longer determine the world in which we live.

The failure of the diplomats of 1919—a failure that no

one has since been able to repair, whose results we have lived with ever since—has been a terribly mixed legacy. The rise of Hitler, the Second World War, the riots and revolutions that plague a world without political order have been the cause of enormous bloodshed and suffering. Yet, at the same time, the collapse of the old order was a necessary prelude to the spread of self-rule, the liberation of new nations and classes, the release of new freedom and independence. The old order was, finally, an ally of old privilege, a fossil of the nineteenth century, a relic of a clockwork universe that had gone out of existence forever.

# Glossary of Important Participants

**For the Allied and Associative Powers**

**Georges Clemenceau:** Premier of the French Third Republic (1917–1919); one of the Big Three Allied leaders.

**Marshal Ferdinand Foch:** French officer and head of the Allied armed forces at the close of World War I.

**Colonel Edward House:** Woodrow Wilson's chief adviser at the peace conference.

**John Maynard Keynes:** Young economist and adviser to British negotiators.

**David Lloyd George:** Prime minister of Great Britain (1916–1922); one of the Big Three Allied leaders.

**Vittorio Orlando:** Prime minister of Italy in 1919; hoped to exert strong influence at the Paris Peace Conference.

**General John Pershing:** Head of American forces in Europe at the end of World War I.

**Raymond Poincarè:** President of the French Third Republic and host of the Paris Peace Conference.

**General Jan Smuts:** British South African officer and important British negotiator.

**Woodrow Wilson:** President of the United States (1912–1920); author of the Fourteen Points and creator of the League of Nations; one of the Big Three Allied leaders.

**For Germany**

**Gustav Bauer:** Replaced Philipp Scheidemann as prime minister of the Weimar Republic shortly before the signing of the treaty.

**Count Ulrich von Brockdorff-Rantzau:** Head of the original German delegation to the Paris Peace Conference.

**Friedrich Ebert:** President of the Weimar Republic (1918–1925).

**Matthias Erzberger:** Minister of finance and head of the German Catholic Center Party.

**Field Marshal Paul von Hindenburg:** Titular head of the German armed forces.

**General Erich Ludendorff:** Effective head of the German army at the end of World War I.

**Prince Max of Baden:** Asked for the November 1918 armistice ending World War I.

**Philipp Scheidemann:** First prime minister of the Weimar Republic; resigned due to disagreements over the treaty.

# For Further Research

## Books

Louis Auchincloss, *Woodrow Wilson*. New York: Viking Penguin, 2000.

Thomas A. Bailey, *Wilson and the Peacemakers*. New York: Macmillan, 1947.

Norman H. Baynes, ed., *The Speeches of Adolf Hitler*. New York: Howard Fertig, 1969.

Winston S. Churchill, *The Second World War*. Vol. 1. *The Gathering Storm*. London: Cassell, 1948.

———, *The World Crisis, 1912–1918: The Aftermath*. London: T. Butterworth, 1931.

Georges Clemenceau: *Grandeur and Misery of Victory*. New York: Harcourt Brace, 1930.

George Creel, *The War, the World, and Wilson*. New York: Harper and Brothers, 1920.

Gregor Dallas, *At the Heart of a Tiger: Clemenceau and His World*. New York: Carroll and Graf, 1993.

E.J. Dillon, *The Inside Story of the Peace Conference*. New York: Harper and Brothers, 1920.

Michael L. Dockrill and J. Douglas Goold, *Peace Without Promise: Britain and the Peace Conferences, 1919–23*. Hamden, CT: Archon Books, 1981.

Howard Elcock, *Portrait of a Decision: The Council of Four and the Treaty of Versailles*. London: Eyre Methuen, 1972.

Matthias Erzberger, *The League of Nations: The Way to the World's Peace*. New York: Henry Holt, 1919.

Richard Garrett, *The Final Betrayal: The Armistice 1918 and Afterwards*. Sheffield, Southampton, UK: Buchan and Enright, 1989.

Peter Gay, *Weimar Culture*. New York: Harper Torchbooks, 1968.

Robert C. Goldstein, *The Road Between the Wars*. New York: Dial, 1978.

Robert Graves, *Goodbye to All That*. London: J. Cape, 1929.

Ruth B. Henig, *The Weimar Republic, 1919–33*. London: Routledge, 1998.

Adolf Hitler, *Mein Kampf.* Boston: Houghton Mifflin, 1943.

John Maynard Keynes, *The Economic Consequences of the Peace.* New York: Harcourt, Brace, and Howe, 1920.

Thomas J. Knock, *To End All Wars: Woodrow Wilson and the Quest for a New World Order.* New York: Oxford University Press, 1992.

David Lloyd George, *Memoirs of the Peace Conference.* New York: H. Fertig, 1972.

———, *Where Are We Going?* New York: George H. Doran, 1923.

Charles L. Mee Jr., *The End of Order: Versailles, 1919.* New York: E.P. Dutton, 1980.

Samuel W. Mitcham Jr., *Why Hitler? The Genesis of the Nazi Reich.* Westport, CT: Praeger, 1996.

Harold Nicolson, *Peacemaking, 1919.* Boston: Houghton Mifflin, 1933.

Philipp Scheidemann, *The Making of the New Germany: The Memoirs of Philipp Scheidemann.* New York: D. Appleton, 1929.

Gerhard Schulz, *Revolutions and Peace Treaties.* London: Methuen, 1967.

William L. Shirer, *The Rise and Fall of the Third Reich.* New York: Fawcett Crest, 1950.

Raymond Jones Sontag, *European Diplomatic History, 1871–1932.* New York: Appleton Century Crofts, 1933.

H.W.V. Temperley, ed., *A History of the Peace Conference of Paris.* London: Henrey Frowde, 1920.

# Index